The Pursuit of God

In Modern Language
A.W. Tozer

NOBLE
&TRUE
BOOKS

Contents

Preface

In this time of almost universal darkness, there is one encouraging glimmer: within conservative Christianity, more and more people are experiencing a deep hunger for God. They seek genuine spiritual realities and won't settle for mere words or with correct "interpretations" of truth. Their thirst for God drives them to drink deeply from the Fountain of Living Water.

This might be the only genuine sign of revival that I've noticed within the religious landscape. It's like a small cloud on the horizon—a sign that a few saints have been eagerly anticipating. If embraced, it could bring new life to many souls and rekindle the awe and wonder that should accompany faith in Christ. Sadly, that wonder seems to have faded from the Church of God in our time.

Religious leaders need to recognize this hunger. In today's evangelicalism, it's like we've set up an altar and divided the sacrifice, but we're content rearranging the pieces without noticing that there's no fire atop lofty Carmel. Thankfully, a few care deeply. They love the altar and the sacrifice, but they can't accept the ongoing absence of fire. Their thirst is for God above all else—they long to experience the profound love of Christ, as foretold by the prophets and sung by the psalmists.

Today, we have no shortage of Bible teachers who accurately explain the principles of Christ's doctrines. However, many of them focus solely on teaching the basics of the faith year after year, oblivious to the fact that their ministry lacks a tangible sense of God's presence. Their personal lives show nothing out of the ordinary. Meanwhile, the believers they serve still carry an unfulfilled longing that their teaching fails to address.

In our pulpits today, there's a real lack. Just as Milton said, "The hungry sheep look up, and are not fed." It's a solemn scandal in God's Kingdom to see His children starving while sitting at the Father's table. And Wesley's wisdom holds true: "Orthodoxy, or right opinion, is, at best, a very slender part of religion. Though right tempers cannot subsist without right opinions, yet right opinions may subsist without right tempers. There may be a right opinion of God without either love or one right temper toward Him. Satan is a proof of this."

Thanks to our Bible societies and other effective agencies, there are now millions of people who hold 'right opinions' about faith—perhaps more than ever before in Church history. Yet, I wonder if true spiritual worship has ever been at a lower ebb. In many sections of the Church, the art of worship has been lost, replaced by a strange thing called the 'program.' This borrowed term, originally from the stage, now characterizes what passes for worship.

While sound Bible exposition is essential, it can sometimes leave hearers spiritually malnourished. For it is not mere words that nourish the soul, but God Himself, and unless and until the hearers find God in personal experience they are no better for having heard the truth. The Bible is not an end in itself, but a means to bring men to an intimate and satisfying knowledge of God, that they may enter into Him, that they may delight in His Presence, may taste and know the inner sweetness of the very God Himself in the core and center of their hearts.

This book aims to help hungry souls find God. It's not entirely new; others have explored these holy mysteries. But even if my fire isn't grand, it's genuine. Perhaps some can light their candle from its flame.

A. W. Tozer

Chicago, Ill.

June 16, 1948

Following Hard after God

My soul follows close behind You; Your right hand upholds me. Ps. 63:8

Christian theology teaches the concept of prevenient grace. Simply put, before a person seeks God, God has already sought them.

Before a sinful person can even form a right thought about God, there must have been an enlightening work within him. Imperfect though it may be, this work is the true cause behind all subsequent desires, seeking, and prayers.

We pursue God solely because He has ignited an urge within us, compelling us to seek Him. Our Lord Himself declared, "No one can come to me unless the Father who sent me draws them." Through this prevenient drawing, God removes any credit from us for the act of coming to Him. The initial impulse to pursue God originates with Him, but as we ardently follow after Him, we remain securely in His hand: "Your right hand upholds me."

In this divine "sustaining" and human "following", there is no contradiction. Everything originates from God, for as von Hügel teaches, *God is always the initiator*. In practice, however (when God's prior work meets our present response), we must actively pursue God. On our part, there must be genuine reciprocation if this secret drawing of God is to result in a tangible experience of the Divine. As stated with personal feeling in Psalm 42, "As the deer pants for the water brooks, So pants my soul for You, O

God. My soul thirsts for God, for the living God. When shall I come and appear before God?" This is deep calling unto deep, and the longing heart will understand it.

The doctrine of justification by faith, a Biblical truth that liberates us from legalism and futile self-effort, has unfortunately been misunderstood in our time. Some interpretations have even hindered people from truly knowing God. The whole transaction of religious conversion has been made mechanical and spiritless. Faith may now be exercised without a significant change to your moral life and without embarrassment to the Adamic ego. Christ may be "received" without creating any special love for Him in the soul of the receiver. The man is "saved," but he is not hungry or thirsty after God. In fact he is specifically taught to be satisfied and encouraged to be content with little.

In the same way that the modern scientist has lost God amid the wonders of His world; we Christians are in real danger of losing God amid the wonders of His Word. We have almost forgotten that God is a Person and, as such, our relationship to Him can be cultivated as with another person. It is a fundamental part of being a person to be able to understand other people. However, gaining full knowledge of one person by another cannot happen in a single interaction. It is only through longed and loving engagement that the full potential of both can be explored.

All social interaction between people is a response of one person to another, ranging from the most casual encounter between individuals to the deepest, most intimate connection the human soul can experience. Genuine religion is, at its core, the response of created personalities to the Creating Personality, God. John 17:3 states, "And this is eternal life, that they may know You, the only true God, and Jesus Christ whom You have sent."

God is a Person, and in the deep of His mighty nature He thinks, wills, enjoys, feels, loves, desires, and suffers as any other person may. In making Himself known to us, God follows the familiar pattern of personal inter- action. He communicates with us through the pathways of our minds, our wills, and our emotions. The ongoing and unhindered exchange of love and thought between God and the soul of the redeemed person is the beating heart of New Testament religion.

This interaction between God and the individual soul is known to us through conscious personal awareness. It is personal - it does not come through the collective body of believers, but is known to the individual, and to the group through the individuals who make it up. And it is con- scious - it does not remain below the level of consciousness and work there unseen by the soul (as some believe infant baptism does), but comes within the field of awareness where the person can "know" it just as they know any other fact of experience.

You and I are on a small scale (apart from our sins) what God is on a large scale. Being made in His image, we have within us the capacity to know Him. In our sins, we lack only the power. The moment the Spirit has brought us to life through rebirth, our entire being senses its kinship to God and responds with joyful recognition. This is the heavenly birth without which we cannot see the Kingdom of God. However, it is not an endpoint, but a beginning, for now starts the glorious pursuit, the heart's happy exploration of the infinite riches of the Godhead. That is where we start, I say, but where we end, no one has yet discovered, for within the awe-inspiring and mysterious depths of the Triune God, there is neither limit nor end.

Shoreless Ocean, who can sound Thee?

Thine own eternity is round Thee,

Majesty divine!

To have found God and still to pursue Him is the soul's paradox of love, scorned indeed by those who are too-easily-satisfied, but justified in happy experience by the children of the burning heart. St. Bernard stated this holy paradox in a musical quatrain that will be instantly understood by every worshipping soul:

We taste Thee, O Thou Living Bread,

And long to feast upon Thee still:

We drink of Thee, the Fountainhead

And thirst our souls from Thee to fill.

Engage with the holy men and women of the past, and you will soon feel the intensity of their desire for God. They mourned for Him, they prayed and wrestled and sought for Him day and night, without ceasing, and when they had found Him, the discovery was all the sweeter for the long seeking. Moses used the fact that he knew God as an argument for knowing Him better. "Now therefore, I pray you, if I have found favor in your sight, show me now your way, that I may know you and find favor in your sight"; and from there he rose to make the bold request, "I beseech you, show me your glory." God was openly pleased by this display of passion, and the next day called Moses into the mountain, and there solemnly caused all His glory to pass before him.

David's life was a torrent of spiritual longing, and his psalms resound with the cry of the seeker and the joyful shout of the finder. Paul confessed that the driving force of his life was his burning desire for Christ. "That I may know Him" was the goal of his heart, and to this he sacrificed everything. "Yet indeed I also count all things loss for the excellence of the knowledge of Christ Jesus my Lord, for whom I have suffered the loss of all things, and count them as rubbish, that I may gain Christ".

Hymns are sweet with the longing for God, the God whom, even as the singer seeks, they know they have already found. "His track I see and I'll pursue," sang our ancestors but that song is no longer heard in the congregation. How tragic that in this dark time, we have had our seeking done for us by our teachers. Everything is made to center on the initial act of "accepting" Christ (a term, by the way, that is not found in the Bible), and we are not expected to crave any further revelation of God to our souls thereafter. We have been ensnared in the coils of a flawed logic that insists that if we have found Him, we need seek Him no more. This is presented to us as the pinnacle of orthodoxy, and it is taken for granted that no Bible-taught Christian ever believed otherwise. Thus, the entire testimony of the worshipping, seeking, singing Church on that subject is abruptly set aside. The experiential, heart-centered theology of a vast army of fragrant saints is rejected in favor of a smug interpretation of Scripture that would have sounded strange to an Augustine, a Rutherford, or a Brainerd.

In the midst of this great chill there are some, I rejoice to acknowledge, who will not be content with shallow logic. They will acknowledge the power of the argument, and then turn away with tears to seek out some solitary place and pray, "O God, show me your glory." They want to taste, to touch with their hearts, to see with their inner eyes the wonder that is God.

I want to deliberately encourage this mighty longing after God. The lack of it has brought us to our present low estate. The stiff and wooden quality about our religious lives is a result of our lack of holy desire. Complacency is a deadly foe of all spiritual growth. Acute desire must be present or there will be no manifestation of Christ to His people. He waits to be wanted. Too bad that with many of us He waits so long, so very long, in vain.

Every era has its own distinctive qualities. Right now, we are in a time of religious complexity. The simplicity that is in Christ is rarely found among us. Instead, we have programs, methods, organizations, and a whirlwind of anxious activities that occupy our time and attention but can never fulfill the yearning of the heart. The shallowness of our inner lives, the emptiness of our worship, and the slavish imitation of the world that characterizes our promotional techniques all testify that we, in this day, know God only incompletely, and the peace of God scarcely at all.

If we want to find God amidst all the religious externals, we must first resolve to seek Him, and then proceed in a spirit of simplicity. Now as always, God reveals Himself to "babes", and conceals Himself from the wise and prudent. We must simplify our approach to Him. We must strip away non-essentials (and they will be found to be wonderfully few). We must abandon all effort to impress, and come with the guileless openness of a child. If we do this, without doubt God will respond quickly.

When religion has said its last word, there is little that we need other than God Himself. The evil habit of seeking *God-and* effectively prevents us from finding God in full revelation. In the "and" lies our great woe. If we omit the "and" we shall soon find God, and in Him we shall find that for which we have all our lives been secretly longing.

We need not fear that in seeking God only we may narrow our lives or restrict the motions of our expanding hearts. The opposite is true. We can well afford to make God our All, to concentrate, to sacrifice the many for the One.

The author of the quaint old English classic, *The Cloud of Unknowing*, teaches us how to do this. "Lift up thine heart unto God with a meek stirring of love; and mean Himself, and none of His goods. And thereto, look thee loath to think on aught but God Himself. So that nought work in thy wit, nor in thy will, but only God Himself. This is the work of the soul that most pleaseth God."

Again, he recommends that in prayer we practice a further stripping down of everything, even of our theology. "For it sufficeth enough, a naked intent direct unto God without any other cause than Himself." Yet underlying all his thinking was the solid foundation of New Testament truth, for he explains that by "Himself" he means God who created you, redeemed you, and graciously called you to your position. If we would have religion wrapped and folded into one word, so that you may better grasp it, take a little word of one syllable - for so it is better than one of two syllables, for the shorter it is, the better it aligns with the work of the Spirit. And such a word is this GOD or this LOVE.

When the Lord divided Canaan among the tribes of Israel, Levi received no share of the land. God said to him simply, "I am your portion and your inheritance," and by those words made him richer than all his brethren, richer than all the kings and rajas who have ever lived in the world. And there is a spiritual principle here, a principle still valid for every priest of the Most High God.

The man who has God for his treasure has all things in One. Many common treasures may be denied him, or if he is allowed to have them, the pleasure of them will be so moderated that they will never be essential to his happiness. Or if he must watch them slip away, one by one, he will hardly feel a sense of loss, for possessing the Source of all things, he has in the One all fulfillment, all pleasure, all delight. Whatever he may lose, he has truly lost nothing, for now he has it all in the One, and he has it purely, rightly, and forever.

O God, I have tasted your goodness, and it has both satisfied me and made me thirsty for more. I am painfully conscious of my need of further grace. I am ashamed of my lack of desire. O God, the Triune God, I want to want you; I long to be filled with longing; I thirst to be made more thirsty still. Show me your glory, I pray, so that I may know you indeed. Begin in mercy a new work of love in me. Say to my soul, "Rise up, my love, my fair one, and come away." Then give me grace to rise and follow you up from this misty lowland where I have wandered so long. In Jesus' Name, Amen.

Study Guide

The author speaks of a "deep hunger for God." Have you experienced this? How would you describe it? How is it different from simply following religious practices?

Read Psalm 42. How does the psalmist express their hunger for God? List specific phrases that resonate with you.

Choose one day this week to fast from a distraction (e.g., social media, television) and use that time to "seek God's face." Write about your experience here:

> "The man is "saved," but he is not hungry or thirsty after God. In fact, he is specifically taught to be satisfied and encouraged to be content with little."

What does the phrase "taught to be satisfied and encouraged to be content with little" mean in the context of modern Christianity? Can you think of examples where this might be happening in churches today? ᵖ⁴

How do you understand the difference between knowing about God and knowing God personally? How might this difference impact your spiritual life?

The author speaks of an "urge" put within us by God that spurs us to pursue Him. Have you felt this urge? How would you describe it?

Examine John 6:44-45. How does Jesus describe the Father's role in drawing people to Himself?

"The impulse to pursue God originates with God, but the outworking of that impulse is our following hard after Him."

How do you understand the balance between God's initiative and our response in pursuing a relationship with Him?

Record daily how you've pursued God and how you've sensed Him pursuing you. Reflect on the balance between His initiative and your response.

Personal Reflection and Journal

Use this space to write your responses, insights, and experiences as you work through this study. Consider the following prompts:

- What new understanding of "pursuing God" have I gained?

- How has my hunger for God deepened or changed?

- What obstacles am I facing in seeking a more intimate knowledge of God?

"Lord, awaken in me a deeper hunger for Your presence. Like the psalmist, may my soul pant for You as the deer pants for streams of water. Show me where I might be 'rearranging pieces' in my spiritual life without experiencing Your fire. Ignite a passion in me for genuine encounter with You. Guide me as I read Your Word. Help me to see beyond the words on the page to the living God they reveal. May my Bible study lead me into an intimate knowledge of You."

The Blessedness of Possessing Nothing

Blessed are the poor in spirit: for theirs is the kingdom of heaven. Matt. 5:3

Before the Lord God made man upon the earth He first prepared for him by creating a world of useful and pleasant things for his sustenance and delight. In the Genesis account of the creation these are called simply "things." They were made for man's uses, but they were meant always to be external to the man and subservient to him. At the innermost core of the man was a sacred space where none but God was worthy to enter. Within him was God; outside, a thousand gifts which God had bestowed upon him.

But sin has introduced complications and has made those very gifts of God a potential source of ruin to the soul.

Our woes began when God was forced out of His central space and "things" were allowed to enter. In the human heart "things" have taken over. By nature, men now have no peace in their hearts, for God is no longer crowned there. In the moral dusk of the heart stubborn and aggressive usurpers fight among themselves for first place on the throne.

This is not a mere metaphor, but an accurate analysis of our real spiritual trouble. There is within the human heart a tough fibrous root of fallen nature that is driven to possess, always to possess. It craves "things" with a deep and fierce passion. The words "my" and "mine" may look innocent enough on the page, but their constant and widespread use is telling. They express the real nature of the old Adamic man better than a thousand volumes of theology could do. They are verbal symptoms of our deep disease. The roots of our hearts have grown down into "things", and we dare not pull up one little root or we think we will die. "Things" have become necessary to us, a development never originally intended. God's gifts now take the place of God, and the whole course of nature is upset by the monstrous substitution.

Our Lord referred to this tyranny of "things" when He said to His disciples, "If any man will come after me, let him deny himself, and take up his cross, and follow me. For whosoever will save his life shall lose it: and whosoever shall lose his life for my sake shall find it."

To break this truth into more understandable pieces, it would seem there is within each of us an enemy that we endanger ourselves by tolerating. Jesus called it "life" and "self," or as we would say, the "self-life". Its defining feature is its possessiveness: the words "gain" and "profit" point to this. To let this enemy live is ultimately to lose everything. To reject it and surrender all for Christ's sake is to lose nothing in the end, but to preserve everything unto eternal life. Here we are given a hint to the only effective way to destroy this foe: it is by the Cross. "Let him take up his cross and follow me."

The way to deeper knowledge of God is through the lonely valleys of soul poverty and renunciation of all things. he blessed ones who inherit the Kingdom are those who have rejected every external thing and uprooted from their hearts all sense of possession. These are the "poor in spirit." They have reached an inward state mirroring the outward circumstances of the common beggar on the streets of Jerusalem; that is the true meaning of the word "poor" as Christ used it. These blessed poor are no longer slaves to the tyranny of "things". They have broken free from the yoke of the oppressor; and they have done this not by fighting, but by surrendering. Though free from all sense of possession, they yet possess all things. "Theirs is the kingdom of heaven."

I urge you to take this seriously. It is not meant to be just another Bible teaching to be filed away in your mind along with a lifeless collection of other doctrines. It is a signpost pointing to richer spiritual grounds, a path carved into the steep slopes of God's mountain. We must not try to bypass it if we want to continue this holy pursuit. We must climb one step at a time. If we refuse even one step, we halt our progress.

As is often the case, this New Testament principle of spiritual life is best illustrated in the Old Testament. The story of Abraham and Isaac provides a powerful image of the surrendered life and serves as an excellent commentary on the first Beatitude.

Abraham was elderly when Isaac was born, old enough to have been his grandfather, and the child instantly became the joy and idol of his heart. From the moment he first awkwardly cradled the tiny form in his arms, he became a devoted love slave to his son. God made a point of noting the strength of this affection. And it's not hard to understand why. The baby represented everything sacred to his father's heart: God's promises, the covenants, the hopes of years, and the long-awaited messianic dream. As he watched Isaac grow from infancy to young adulthood, the old man's heart became more and more entwined with his son's life, until at last their relationship verged on dangerous territory. It was then that God intervened to save both father and son from the consequences of an uncleansed love.

"Take your son," God said to Abraham, "your only son Isaac, whom you love, and go to the land of Moriah; offer him there as a burnt offering on one of the mountains I will show you." The writer spares us the details of

Abraham's agony that night near Beersheba as the old man wrestled with his God, but we can imagine with awe the bent figure struggling alone under the stars. Perhaps not until a Greater than Abraham wrestled in Gethsemane did such pain visit a human soul. If only Abraham himself could have died instead. That would have been a thousand times easier, for he was old now, and death would not have been a great trial for one who had walked so long with God. Besides, it would have been a final sweet comfort to let his fading eyes rest on his strong son who would carry on the family line and fulfill God's promises made long ago in Ur.

How could he kill the boy? Even if he could overcome his wounded and protesting heart, how could he square this act with the promise, "Through Isaac shall your offspring be named"? This was Abraham's trial by fire, and he did not fail the test. While the stars still shone like sharp white points above the tent where Isaac slept, and long before dawn began to lighten the east, the old saint had made up his mind. He would offer his son as God had instructed, and *then trust God to raise him from the dead*. This, according to Hebrews, was the solution his aching heart found in the dark night, and he rose "early in the morning" to carry out the plan. It's moving to see that, while he was mistaken about God's method, he had correctly sensed the secret of God's great heart. And the solution aligns well with the New Testament teaching, "Whoever loses his life for my sake will find it."

God allowed the suffering old man to go through with it until the point where He knew there was no turning back, then stopped him from harming the boy. To the bewildered patriarch, God essentially says, "It's alright, Abraham. I never meant for you to actually kill the boy. I only wanted to remove him from the center of your heart so I could reign there unchallenged. I wanted to correct the distortion in your love. Now you can have the boy back, safe and sound. Take him and return to your tent. Now I know that you fear God, since you have not withheld your son, your only son, from me."

Then heaven opened and a voice spoke, saying, "By myself I have sworn, declares the Lord, because you have done this and have not withheld your son, your only son, I will surely bless you, and I will multiply your offspring as the stars of heaven and as the sand on the seashore. Your offspring shall possess the gate of his enemies, and in your offspring shall all the nations of the earth be blessed, because you have obeyed my voice."

The old man of God lifted his head to answer the Voice, standing there on the mountain strong, pure, and noble, a man marked by the Lord for special treatment, a friend and favorite of the Most High. Now he was a man fully surrendered, utterly obedient, possessing nothing. He had focused his all in the person of his beloved son, and God had taken it from him. God could have started at the edges of Abraham's life and worked inward to the center; instead, He chose to cut straight to the heart and have it done in one sharp act of separation. This approach was economical in means and time. It hurt terribly, but it was effective.

I've said that Abraham possessed nothing. Yet wasn't this poor man rich? Everything he had owned before was still his to enjoy: sheep, camels, herds, and goods of all kinds. He also had his wife and his friends, and best of all, he had his son Isaac safe beside him. He had everything, but he *possessed nothing*. This is the spiritual secret. This is the sweet theology of the heart that can only be learned in the school of renunciation. The books on systematic theology may overlook this, but the wise will understand.

After that painful yet blessed experience, I think the words "my" and "mine" never meant the same to Abraham again. The sense of ownership they imply was gone from his heart. "Things" had been cast out forever. They had become external to him. His inner heart was free from them.

The world said, "Abraham is rich," but the aged patriarch only smiled. He couldn't explain it to them, but he knew he owned nothing, that his real treasures were inward and eternal.

There's no doubt that this possessive clinging to things is one of the most harmful habits in life. Because it's so natural, it's rarely seen for the evil it is; but its effects are tragic.

We're often afraid to give up our treasures to the Lord, fearing for their safety; this is especially true with loved ones. But we needn't fear. Our Lord came not to destroy but to save. Everything we commit to Him is safe, and nothing is really safe that isn't committed to Him.

Our gifts and talents should also be turned over to Him. We should recognize them for what they are, God's loan to us, and never consider them our own. We have no more right to claim credit for special abilities than for blue eyes or strong muscles. "For who makes you different from anyone else? What do you have that you did not receive?"

The Christian who is self-aware enough will recognize the symptoms of this possession sickness, and will be sad to find them in his own heart. If his longing for God is strong enough, he'll want to do something about it. So, what should he do?

First, he should stop defending himself and not try to make excuses either to himself or to the Lord. Whoever defends himself will have only himself as a defense, but let him come defenseless before the Lord and he'll have God Himself as his defender. Let the seeking Christian trample every slippery trick of his deceitful heart and insist on honest, open relations with the Lord.

Then he should remember that this is serious business. No careless or casual approach will do. Let him come to God fully determined to be heard. Let him insist that God accept his all, that He remove "things" from his heart and reign there in power. He may need to be specific, naming things and people one by one. If he's willing to be drastic enough, he can shorten his struggle from years to minutes and enter the good land long before his slower brothers who coddle their feelings and insist on caution in dealing with God.

Let's not forget that a truth like this can't be learned by memorization as we might learn scientific facts. We must experience it to truly know it. We must live through Abraham's harsh and bitter experiences in our hearts to know the blessing that follows. The ancient curse won't leave painlessly; the tough old miser within us won't lie down and die on command. He must be torn from our heart like a plant from soil; extracted in agony and blood like a tooth from the jaw. He must be forced out of our soul violently, as Christ forced out the money changers from the temple. We'll need to steel ourselves against his pitiful begging, recognizing it as self-pity, one of the worst sins of the human heart.

If we truly want to know God in growing closeness, we must go this way of giving up. And if we're set on pursuing God, He will sooner or later bring us to this test. Abraham didn't know his experience was a test at the time, but if he had chosen differently, the whole Old Testament history would have changed. God would have found His man, surely, but Abraham's loss would have been beyond words. So we'll be brought one by one to the testing place, and we may not know when we're there. At that place, we won't have many choices - just one and an alternative, but our whole future will depend on the choice we make.

Father, I want to know You, but my cowardly heart fears giving up its toys. I can't part with them without inner pain, and I don't try to hide from You the fear of parting. I come trembling, but I do come. Please remove from my heart all those things I've cherished so long that have become part of my very self, so You can enter and live there without rival. Then You'll make the place of Your feet glorious. Then my heart won't need the sun to shine in it, for You'll be its light, and there will be no night there. In Jesus' Name, Amen.

Study Guide

The author suggests that our desire to possess is a "tough fibrous root of fallen life." How do you see this manifesting in your own life? In society?

Study Philippians 3:7-11. How does Paul's attitude reflect the "blessedness of possessing nothing"? What did he consider "loss" for the sake of Christ?

Reflect on your use of "my" and "mine." How might this reveal your attitude towards possessions and your relationship with God? For one day, try to avoid using these pronouns. How does this change your perspective on what you have?

Examine Luke 14:33. How does Jesus' statement here challenge our understanding of discipleship and possession?

Identify something valuable to you (time, money, or a possession) and give it away as an act of worship. Reflect on how this impacts your relationship with God.

How does the story of Abraham and Isaac illustrate the concept of possessing nothing?

"Everything we commit to Him is safe, and nothing is really safe that isn't committed to Him."

Make a list of your most valued possessions. Pray over each item, asking God to help you hold it loosely and be willing to give it up if He asks.

Personal Reflection and Journal

Use this space to write your responses, insights, and experiences as you work through this study. Consider the following prompts:

- How is God speaking to me about my attachments to possessions or status?

- In what ways am I experiencing a "deeper knowledge of God" through this process?

- What fears or reservations do I have about fully embracing this teaching?

"Lord, reveal to me the areas of my life where I'm clinging too tightly to possessions or status. Help me to hold all things loosely for Your sake. Give me the courage to follow You even when it means letting go of things I hold dear. Like Abraham, may I trust You completely. Lead me into the 'lonely valleys of soul poverty' that I might know God more deeply. Help me find joy in possessing nothing but You."

Removing the Veil

Therefore, brethren, having boldness to enter the Holiest by the blood of Jesus.
Heb. 10:19

Among the well-known sayings of Church leaders, none is more famous than Augustine's, "You have made us for Yourself, and our hearts are restless until they find rest in You."

The great saint sums up in these few words the origin and inner story of humanity. God created us for Himself: this is the only explanation that satisfies the *heart* of a thinking person, no matter what their uncontrolled reason might say. If poor education and twisted thinking lead someone to think otherwise, there's little any Christian can do for them. I have no message for such a person. My words are for those who have already been taught secretly by God's wisdom; I speak to thirsty hearts whose longings have been stirred by God's touch within them. These people don't need logical proof. Their restless hearts provide all the evidence they need.

God made us for Himself. The Shorter Catechism, approved by church leaders at Westminster, asks the age-old questions of what and why. It answers them in one brief sentence, unmatched by any non-inspired work: "Question: What is the main purpose of humanity? Answer: Humanity's main purpose is to glorify God and enjoy Him forever."

This agrees with the twenty-four elders who bow down to worship the eternal God, saying, "You are worthy, Lord, to receive glory, honor, and power: for you created all things, and they exist and were created for your pleasure."

God created us for His enjoyment, and made us so that we, like Him, can enjoy the sweet and mysterious blending of similar personalities in divine fellowship. He meant for us to see Him, live with Him, and draw our life from His smile. But we've been guilty of the "foul revolt" Milton mentions when describing Satan's rebellion. We've broken away from God. We've stopped obeying or loving Him and, in guilt and fear, have run as far as possible from His Presence.

Yet who can escape His Presence when even the highest heavens can't contain Him? As Solomon wisely said, "the Spirit of the Lord fills the world." God's being everywhere is one thing, a solemn fact essential to His perfection. His visible Presence is something else entirely, and it's from this Presence we've fled, like Adam hiding among the garden trees, or like Peter shrinking away saying, "Leave me, Lord, for I'm a sinful man."

So human life on earth is a life away from the Presence, torn from that "blissful center" which is our rightful home, our original state we didn't keep. Losing this is the reason for our constant restlessness.

God's whole work in redemption is to undo the tragic results of that foul revolt, and to bring us back into a right and eternal relationship with Himself. This required dealing with our sins properly, achieving full reconciliation, and opening the way for us to return to conscious fellowship with God and live again in the Presence as before. Then, by His work within us, He moves us to return. We first notice this when our restless hearts feel a longing for God's Presence and we say to ourselves, "I will get up and go to my Father." That's the first step, and as the Chinese sage Lao-tze said, "The journey of a thousand miles begins with a first step."

The inner journey of the soul from the wilderness of sin to enjoying God's Presence is beautifully shown in the Old Testament tabernacle. The returning sinner first entered the outer court, offering a blood sacrifice on the bronze altar and washing in the nearby basin. Then, through a curtain, he entered the holy place where no natural light came, but the golden lampstand, representing Jesus the Light of the World, cast a soft glow. There was also the bread of the Presence, symbolizing Jesus the Bread of Life, and the incense altar, representing constant prayer.

Though the worshipper had experienced much, he hadn't yet entered God's Presence. Another curtain separated the Most Holy Place, where God Himself dwelt above the mercy seat in awe-inspiring glory. While the tabernacle stood, only the high priest could enter there, once a year, with blood for his own and the people's sins. This last curtain was torn when Jesus died on the cross, and we're told this opened the way for all worshippers to enter God's Presence directly through a new, living way.

The New Testament agrees with this Old Testament picture. Saved people no longer need to hesitate fearfully to enter the Most Holy Place. God wants us to push forward into His Presence and live our whole lives there. This isn't just something to know about, but to experience consciously. It's more than a belief to hold; it's a life to enjoy every moment of every day.

This Flame of the Presence was the heart of the Levitical system. Without it, all the tabernacle's furnishings were like words in an unknown language; they meant nothing to Israel or us. The most important fact about the tabernacle was that God was there; a Presence waited behind the curtain. Similarly, God's Presence is central to Christianity. At Christianity's core is God Himself, waiting for His redeemed children to push into conscious awareness of His Presence. Today's popular Christianity only knows this Presence in theory. It doesn't emphasize the Christian's right to experience it now. It teaches we're in God's Presence positionally, but says nothing about needing to actually experience that Presence. The fiery drive that motivated men like McCheyne is completely missing. Today's Christians measure themselves by this flawed standard. Unworthy contentment replaces burning passion. We're satisfied with our legal standing and hardly bother about our lack of personal experience.

Who is this behind the curtain, dwelling in fiery displays? It's none other than God Himself, "One God the Father Almighty, Maker of heaven and earth, of all things visible and invisible," and "One Lord Jesus Christ, the only begotten Son of God; begotten of His Father before all worlds, God from God, Light from Light, Very God of Very God; begotten, not made; being of one substance with the Father," and "the Holy Spirit, the Lord and Giver of life, Who proceeds from the Father and the Son, Who with the Father and the Son is worshipped and glorified." Yet this holy Trinity is One God, for "we worship one God in Trinity, and Trinity in Unity; not mixing up the Persons, nor dividing the Substance. For there is one Person of the Father, another of the Son, and another of the Holy Spirit. But the Godhead of the Father, Son, and Holy Spirit is all one: equal in glory and co-eternal in majesty." So say the ancient creeds, and so declares the inspired Word.

Behind the curtain is God, the God for whom the world has strangely and inconsistently longed, "if perhaps they might find Him." He has revealed Himself somewhat in nature, but more fully in the Incarnation; now He waits to show Himself in overwhelming fullness to the humble and pure in heart.

The world is dying from lack of knowing God and the Church is starving for want of His Presence. The quick fix for most of our religious problems would be to enter the Presence in spiritual experience, to suddenly realize we are in God and God is in us. This would lift us out of our sad narrowness and expand our hearts. This would burn away the impurities from our lives like the insects and fungi were burned away by the fire in the bush.

What a vast world to explore, what an ocean to swim in is this God and Father of our Lord Jesus Christ. He is eternal, meaning He existed before time and is completely independent of it. Time began in Him and will end in Him. He pays no tribute to it and suffers no change from it. He is unchangeable, meaning He has never changed and can never change in the slightest. To change, He would need to go from better to worse or from worse to better. He can't do either, for being perfect He can't become more perfect, and if He became less perfect He would be less than God. He is all-knowing, meaning He knows in one effortless act all matter, spirit, relationships, and events. He has no past and no future. He is, and none of the limiting terms used for creatures apply to Him. Love, mercy, and righteousness are His, and holiness so indescribable that no comparisons can express it. Only fire can give a hint of it. In fire He appeared at the burning bush; in the pillar of fire He lived through the long wilderness journey. The fire that glowed between the cherubim's wings in the holy place was called the "shekinah," the Presence, through Israel's glory years, and when the Old gave way to the New, He came at Pentecost as a fiery flame and rested on each disciple.

Spinoza wrote about the intellectual love of God, and he was partly right. But the highest love of God isn't intellectual, it's spiritual. God is spirit and only the human spirit can truly know Him. Deep in a person's spirit, the fire must glow or their love isn't real love for God. The greatest people in God's Kingdom have been those who loved God more than others did. We know who they were and happily honor the depth and sincerity of their devotion. We only need to pause briefly and their names parade past us, fragrant with precious perfumes from royal palaces.

Frederick Faber was one whose soul longed for God like a deer longs for streams of water. The way God revealed Himself to Faber's seeking heart set his whole life on fire with a burning worship rivaling that of the angels before God's throne. His love for God included all three Persons of the Trinity equally, yet he seemed to have a special kind of love for each One. About God the Father, he sings:

Only to sit and think of God,

Oh what a joy it is!

To think the thought, to breathe the Name;

Earth has no higher bliss.

Father of Jesus, love's reward!

What rapture will it be,

Prostrate before Thy throne to lie,

And gaze and gaze on Thee!

His love for Christ was so strong that it almost overwhelmed him. It burned inside him like a sweet and holy passion, and poured from his lips like melted gold. In one of his sermons he says, "Wherever we turn in the church of God, there is Jesus. He is the beginning, middle and end of everything to us.... There is nothing good, nothing holy, nothing beautiful, nothing joyous which He is not to His servants. No one need be poor, because, if he chooses, he can have Jesus for his own property and possession. No one need be downcast, for Jesus is the joy of heaven, and it is His joy to enter into sorrowful hearts. We can exaggerate about many things; but we can never exaggerate our obligation to Jesus, or the compassionate abundance of the love of Jesus to us. All our lives long we might talk of Jesus, and yet we should never come to an end of the sweet things that might be said of Him. Eternity will not be long enough to learn all He is, or to praise Him for all He has done, but then, that matters not; for we shall be always with Him, and we desire nothing more." And addressing our Lord directly he says to Him:

I love Thee so, I know not how

My transports to control;

Thy love is like a burning fire

Within my very soul.

Faber's intense love also included the Holy Spirit. He didn't just recognize the Spirit's divinity and equality with the Father and Son in his beliefs, but he constantly celebrated it in his songs and prayers. He would literally bow his head to the ground in his passionate worship of the Third Person of the Trinity. In one of his powerful hymns to the Holy Spirit, he summarizes his deep devotion like this:

O Spirit, beautiful and dread!

My heart is fit to break

With love of all Thy tenderness

For us poor sinners' sake.

I've risked boring you with quotes to clearly show what I'm trying to say: God is so amazingly wonderful, so completely delightful that He alone, without anything else, can meet and overflow the deepest needs of our whole nature, as mysterious and deep as that nature is. The kind of worship Faber knew (and he's just one of countless others) can never come from merely knowing facts about God. Hearts that are "ready to break" with love for God are those who have been in His Presence and have seen His majesty with open eyes. These people with breaking hearts had a quality unknown to ordinary people. They spoke with spiritual authority. They had been in God's Presence and reported what they saw. They were prophets, not scribes, because scribes tell what they've read, but prophets tell what they've seen.

This difference is real. Between the scribe who has read and the prophet who has seen, there's a gap as wide as the ocean. Today we have too many orthodox scribes, but where are the prophets? The harsh voice of the scribe echoes across the evangelical world, but the Church waits for the gentle voice of the saint who has passed through the veil and gazed upon the Wonder that is God. Yet, to pass through, to push into living experience of the holy Presence, is a privilege open to every child of God.

With the veil removed by Jesus' sacrifice, with nothing on God's side stopping us from entering, why do we wait outside? Why do we agree to stay just outside the Most Holy Place all our lives and never enter to see God? We hear the Bridegroom say, "Let me see your face, let me hear your voice; for your voice is sweet, and your face is lovely." We feel the call is for us, but we still don't come near, and the years pass and we grow old and tired in the outer courts. What's holding us back?

The usual answer, that we're simply "cold," doesn't explain everything. There's something more serious than a cold heart, something that might be behind that coldness and cause it. What is it? It's the presence of a veil in our hearts. This veil wasn't removed like the first one was, but stays there, blocking out light and hiding God's face from us. It's the veil of our sinful human nature living on, unjudged within us, not crucified or rejected. It's the tightly woven veil of self-centeredness that we've never truly admitted to, that we've been secretly ashamed of, and so have never brought to the cross for judgment. This veil isn't too mysterious or hard to spot. We just need to look in our own hearts and we'll see it there, maybe stitched up and patched, but still there, an enemy to our lives and a real obstacle to our spiritual growth.

This veil isn't pretty and it's not something we usually like to talk about. But I'm speaking to those who deeply want to follow God, and I know they won't turn back just because the path goes through some dark places for a while. God's pull within them will keep them going. They'll face the hard truths and bear the cross for the joy that's coming. So I'll boldly name the threads that make up this inner veil.

It's woven from the fine threads of self-centeredness, the compound sins of the human spirit. These aren't things we do, they're things we are, and that's what makes them so subtle and powerful.

To be clear, these self-sins include: self-righteousness, self-pity, self-confidence, self-sufficiency, self-admiration, self-love, and many others like them. They're buried so deep in us and are so much a part of who we are that we don't notice them until God's light shines on them. The more obvious forms of these sins - like egotism, showing off, and self-promotion - are strangely accepted in Christian leaders, even in very orthodox circles. They're so common that many people think they're part of the gospel message. I hope it's not too cynical to say that these days, they seem to be required for popularity in some parts of the visible Church. Promoting oneself while pretending to promote Christ is now so common that hardly anyone notices it.

You'd think that learning about human sinfulness and the need for salvation through Christ alone would free us from self-sins. But it doesn't work that way. Self can live unchallenged even at the altar. It can watch Christ die and not be moved. It can fight for Reformed faith, preach eloquently about salvation by grace, and grow stronger in the process. To be honest, it seems to thrive on correct beliefs and feels more at home in a Bible conference than in a bar. Even our desire for God can give it a perfect environment to grow.

Self is the dark veil hiding God's face from us. It can only be removed through spiritual experience, not just by learning. You might as well try to teach leprosy out of our bodies. God must destroy it before we're free. We must let the cross do its deadly work in us. We must bring our self-sins to the cross for judgment. We must prepare for suffering somewhat like our Savior experienced under Pontius Pilate.

Remember: when we talk about tearing the veil, we're using a figure of speech that sounds poetic, almost nice. But in reality, it's not nice at all. In human experience, that veil is made of living spiritual tissue. It's made of the sensitive, quivering stuff that makes up our whole being. To touch it is to touch where we feel pain. Tearing it away hurts us and makes us bleed. To say otherwise is to make the cross not a cross and death not death. Dying is never fun. Ripping through the precious, tender stuff of life is always deeply painful. Yet that's what the cross did to Jesus and what it must do to everyone to set them free.

Let's be careful not to try fixing our inner life ourselves to tear the veil. God must do it all. We just need to yield and trust. We must admit, abandon, and reject the self-life, and consider it crucified. But we must distinguish between lazy "acceptance" and God's real work. We must insist the work be done. We can't be satisfied with a neat theory of self-crucifixion. That's like Saul sparing the best animals.

Insist the work be truly done and it will be. The cross is harsh and deadly, but it works. It doesn't keep its victim hanging forever. There comes a time when its work is done and the suffering victim dies. After that comes resurrection glory and power, and the pain is forgotten for the joy of the veil being removed and entering God's Presence in real spiritual experience.

Lord, Your ways are excellent, and human ways are twisted and dark. Show us how to die, so we may rise to new life. Tear the veil of our self-life from top to bottom as You tore the Temple veil. We want to come near with full faith. We want to live with You daily here on earth so we're used to the glory when we enter Your heaven to live with You there. In Jesus' name, Amen.

Study Guide

> "You have made us for Yourself, and our hearts are restless until they find rest in You."

Augustine speaks of our hearts being restless until they find rest in God. How have you experienced this restlessness in your own life?

Read Exodus 33:12-23. How does Moses' desire to see God's glory relate to the theme of this chapter? What can we learn from God's response?

The Westminster Catechism states that our main purpose is to glorify God and enjoy Him forever. How does this align with or challenge your understanding of life's purpose?

Throughout your day, look for glimpses of God's glory in creation, interactions, or circumstances. Keep a "glory journal" to record these moments.

Study 2 Corinthians 3:12-18. How does Paul describe the removal of the veil? What is the result of this removal?

Reflect on what "veils" might be hindering your relationship with God (e.g., sin, misconceptions about God, busyness). Choose one to focus on removing this week.

What do you think the author means by "continuous and unembarrassed interchange of love and thought between God and the soul"? Have you experienced this kind of relationship with God?

Examine Hebrews 10:19-22. How does this passage describe our access to God? How does it relate to the Old Testament tabernacle system?

Study the layout and purpose of the Old Testament tabernacle. Reflect on how Jesus has made it possible for you to enter God's presence freely. How does this impact your approach to God?

Personal Reflection and Journal

Use this space to write your responses, insights, and experiences as you work through this study. Consider the following prompts:

- How is my understanding of God's presence changing through this study?

- What veils do I sense God removing in my life?

- What challenges am I facing in pursuing a more intimate relationship with God?

"Lord, like Augustine, my heart is restless. Help me to find true rest in You alone. Remove any veils that separate me from Your presence. Draw me into a deeper, more intimate relationship with You. Teach me to glorify and enjoy God. Transform my understanding of life's purpose to align with Your truth."

Apprehending God

O taste and see. Ps. 34:8

Over 25 years ago, Canon Holmes from India pointed out that most people's faith in God is based on inference, not reality. For most, God is a conclusion, not a personal experience. They say, "He must exist, so we believe He does." Others know of Him only by hearsay. They've never thought it through themselves, but have heard about Him from others and filed belief in Him away with other bits and pieces of their beliefs. To many, God is just an ideal, another name for goodness, beauty, or truth; or He's law, life, or the creative force behind existence.

These ideas about God vary, but those who hold them share one thing: they don't know God personally. The idea of getting to know Him closely hasn't occurred to them. While they accept His existence, they don't think of Him as knowable like we know things or people.

Christians, in theory, go further than this. Their beliefs require them to believe in God as a person, and they're taught to pray, "Our Father in heaven." Personality and fatherhood suggest the possibility of personal relationship. This is accepted in theory, but for millions of Christians, God is no more real than He is to non-Christians. They go through life trying to love an ideal and be loyal to a mere principle.

Against all this vagueness, the Bible clearly teaches that we can know God personally. A loving Person fills the Bible, walking in the garden and bringing life to every scene. Always, a living Person is there, speaking, pleading, loving, working, and showing Himself whenever His people are open to seeing Him.

The Bible assumes it's obvious that people can know God as directly as they know anything else they experience. It uses the same words to describe knowing God as it does for knowing physical things. "Taste and see that the Lord is good." "All your clothes smell of myrrh, aloes, and cassia, from ivory palaces." "My sheep hear my voice." "Blessed are the pure in heart, for they will see God." These are just four of many such passages. And more important than any single verse is that this is the main message of the whole Scripture.

What can this mean except that we have in our hearts ways to know God as surely as we know physical things through our five senses? We understand the physical world by using the abilities we're given, and we have spiritual abilities to know God and the spiritual world if we follow the Spirit's guidance and start using them.

We assume that a saving work must first happen in the heart. The spiritual abilities of the unsaved person lie dormant, unused and essentially dead; that's the effect of sin on us. The Holy Spirit can awaken these abilities to active life again through rebirth; that's one of the immeasurable benefits of Christ's sacrifice on the cross.

But why do even saved children of God know so little of the constant, conscious communion with God that the Bible seems to offer? The answer is our persistent unbelief. Faith allows our spiritual senses to work. Where faith is weak, the result will be inner numbness towards spiritual things. This is the state of many Christians today. We don't need proof for this. We just need to talk to the first Christian we meet or enter any open church to see it.

A spiritual kingdom surrounds us, within reach of our inner selves, waiting for us to recognize it. God Himself is here waiting for us to respond to His Presence. This eternal world will come alive to us the moment we start to count on its reality.

I've just used two words that need explaining: "count on" and "reality."

By reality, I mean what exists apart from any idea any mind might have of it, and what would exist if there were no minds to think about it. What's real has existence in itself. It doesn't depend on an observer to be valid.

I know some like to mock the average person's idea of reality. They're the idealists who endlessly argue that nothing is real outside the mind. They're the relativists who like to show there are no fixed points in the universe to measure anything from. They look down on us from their intellectual heights and dismiss us as "absolutists." The Christian isn't bothered by this contempt. He can smile back, knowing there's only One who is Absolute: God. But he also knows that the Absolute One has made this world for humans to use, and for all practical purposes of human life, we can act as if things were fixed and real.

Everyone acts this way except the mentally ill. These unfortunate people also struggle with reality, but they're consistent; they insist on living according to their ideas of things. They're honest, and it's their honesty that makes them a social problem.

The idealists and relativists aren't mentally ill. They prove their soundness by living according to the very notions of reality they claim to reject, and by relying on the very fixed points they argue don't exist. They'd earn more respect for their ideas if they lived by them, but they're careful not to. Their ideas are only brain-deep, not life-deep. Whenever real life touches them, they abandon their theories and live like everyone else.

The Christian is too sincere to play with ideas for their own sake. He takes no pleasure in just spinning fancy webs for show. All his beliefs are practical. They're tied into his life. By them he lives or dies, stands or falls for this world and all time to come. He turns away from insincere people.

The sincere person knows the world is real. He finds it when he wakes up, and knows he didn't think it into being. It was here waiting for him when he came, and he knows it will be here to say goodbye when he leaves. Through life's deep wisdom, he's wiser than a thousand doubters. He stands on the earth, feels wind and rain on his face, and knows they're real. He sees the sun by day and stars by night. He sees lightning flash from dark clouds. He hears nature's sounds and human cries of joy and pain. He knows these are real. He sleeps on the cool earth without fear it will vanish. In the morning, the firm ground will be under him, blue sky above, and rocks and trees around him, just like when he closed his eyes. So he lives happily in a real world.

He experiences this real world with his five senses. He understands everything needed for physical life through the abilities God gave him for this world.

By our definition, God is also real. He's real in the absolute, final way that nothing else is. All other reality depends on His. The great Reality is God, who created the lesser, dependent reality of all created things, including us. God exists objectively, separate from any ideas we might have about Him. The worshipping heart doesn't create its Object. It finds Him here when it wakes from its moral sleep in the morning of its rebirth.

We also need to explain the word "count on." This doesn't mean to visualize or imagine. Imagination isn't faith. They're not just different, but opposite. Imagination creates unreal images in the mind and tries to make them seem real. Faith creates nothing; it simply counts on what's already there.

God and the spiritual world are real. We can count on them as surely as we count on the familiar world around us. Spiritual things are there (or rather, here) inviting our attention and challenging our trust.

Our problem is we've developed bad thinking habits. We usually think of the visible world as real and doubt the reality of anything else. We don't deny the spiritual world exists, but we doubt it's real in the usual sense of the word.

The physical world demands our attention constantly throughout our lives. It's loud, insistent, and self-evident. It doesn't ask for our faith; it's here, bombarding our senses, demanding to be accepted as real and final. But sin has clouded our hearts' vision so we can't see that other reality, God's City, shining around us. The physical world wins. The visible becomes the enemy of the invisible; the temporary, of the eternal. That's the curse inherited by every member of Adam's fallen race.

At the core of Christian life is belief in the invisible. The object of Christian faith is unseen reality.

Our uncorrected thinking, influenced by our naturally blind hearts and the intrusive presence of visible things, tends to contrast the spiritual with the real; but no such contrast actually exists. The contrast is elsewhere: between the real and the imaginary, the spiritual and the material, the temporary and the eternal; but never between the spiritual and the real. The spiritual is real.

If we want to rise to the realm of light and power the Bible points us to, we must break the bad habit of ignoring the spiritual. We must shift our focus from the seen to the unseen. The great unseen Reality is God. "Anyone who comes to God must believe that he exists and that he rewards those who earnestly seek him." This is fundamental to a life of faith. From there, we can rise to unlimited heights. Jesus said, "You believe in God; believe also in me." Without the first, there can't be the second.

If we truly want to follow God, we must seek to be other-worldly. I say this knowing that word has been used scornfully by worldly people and applied to Christians as an insult. So be it. Everyone must choose their world. If we who follow Christ, knowing all the facts and what we're doing, deliberately choose God's Kingdom as our focus, I see no reason for anyone to object. If we lose by it, the loss is ours; if we gain, we rob no one. The "other world," which this world looks down on and drunks mock in their songs, is our carefully chosen goal and the object of our holiest desire.

But we must avoid the common mistake of pushing the "other world" into the future. It's not future, but present. It runs alongside our familiar physical world, and the doors between the two worlds are open. The writer to the Hebrews says (in the present tense), "You have come to Mount Zion, to the city of the living God, the heavenly Jerusalem. You have come to thousands of angels in joyful assembly, to the church of the firstborn, whose names are written in heaven. You have come to God, the Judge of all, to the spirits of the righteous made perfect, to Jesus the mediator of a new covenant, and to the sprinkled blood that speaks a better word than the blood of Abel." All these things are contrasted with "the mountain that could be touched" and "the sound of a trumpet and a voice speaking words" that could be heard. Can't we conclude that, just as Mount Sinai's realities were perceived by the senses, Mount Zion's realities are to be grasped by the soul? And this not by imagination, but in actual fact. The soul has eyes to see and ears to hear. They may be weak from long disuse, but Christ's life-giving touch makes them alive now and capable of sharp sight and sensitive hearing.

As we start to focus on God, spiritual things will take shape before our inner eyes. Obeying Christ's word will bring an inner revelation of God

(John 14:21-23). It will give us keen perception, enabling us to see God as promised to the pure in heart. A new awareness of God will take hold of us and we'll begin to taste, hear, and inwardly feel the God who is our life and our all. We'll see the constant shining of the light that gives light to everyone coming into the world. More and more, as our abilities grow sharper and surer, God will become to us the great All, and His Presence the glory and wonder of our lives.

O God, bring to life every power within me, that I may grasp eternal things. Open my eyes that I may see; give me sharp spiritual perception; enable me to taste You and know that You are good. Make heaven more real to me than any earthly thing has ever been. Amen.

Study Guide

> "The Bible assumes it's obvious that people can know God as directly as they know anything else they experience. "

The author suggests that many people's faith in God is based on inference rather than personal experience. How would you describe your own faith? Is it more experiential or intellectual?

Examine your beliefs about God. Which ones are based on personal experience, and which on logical inference? Pray for more experiential knowledge in areas that feel distant.

What does it mean to you to "taste and see" that the Lord is good? How have you experienced this in your life?

As you read Scripture, don't just analyze the text. Instead, try to experience the truths personally. Ask, "How can I taste and see this reality in my life?"

Read Jeremiah 29:13-14. How does this passage relate to the theme of apprehending God? What conditions does God set for being found by us?

"If we want to rise to the realm of light and power the Bible points us to, we must break the bad habit of ignoring the spiritual."

Reflect on how often you think about the spiritual world. What areas of your life do you need to be more aware of spiritual realities? How would a new awareness of God change your daily life?

Personal Reflection and Journal

Use this space to write your responses, insights, and experiences as you work through this study. Consider the following prompts:

- In what ways am I learning to "taste and see" God's goodness?

- How am I experiencing the balance between God's initiative and my response in our relationship?

- What challenges am I facing in developing a more experiential faith?

"Lord, awaken in me a deeper hunger to know You experientially. Help me to 'taste and see' Your goodness in fresh ways. I want to gaze upon You with the eyes of faith. Remove any distractions that pull my attention away from You. Teach me to recognize and respond to Your urging to pursue God. Give me the courage to follow hard after Him."

The Universal Presence

Where can I go from Your Spirit? Or where can I flee from Your presence?
Ps. 139:7

In all Christian teaching, certain basic truths are found. Sometimes they're hidden, often assumed rather than stated, but they're necessary to all truth like primary colors are necessary to a finished painting. One such truth is that God is present everywhere.

God lives in His creation and is everywhere fully present in all His works. Prophets and apostles boldly teach this, and Christian theology generally accepts it. It appears in books, but for some reason, it hasn't sunk into the average Christian's heart to become part of their belief. Christian teachers shy away from its full meaning, and if they mention it at all, they tone it down until it means little. I guess this is because they fear being accused of pantheism; but the teaching of God's presence everywhere is definitely not pantheism.

Pantheism's error is too obvious to fool anyone. It says God is the sum of all created things. Nature and God are one, so touching a leaf or stone is touching God. This, of course, lowers the glory of the unchanging God and, in trying to make all things divine, removes all divinity from the world entirely.

The truth is that while God lives in His world, He is separated from it by a gap that can never be crossed. However closely He may be connected with the work of His hands, they are and must always be different from Him, and He is and must be before them and independent of them. He is above all His works even while He is within them.

What does God being present everywhere mean for Christian experience? It simply means God is here. Wherever we are, God is here. There is no place, there can be no place, where He is not. Ten million intelligent beings standing at as many points in space, separated by unimaginable distances, can each say with equal truth, God is here. No point is closer to God than any other point. It's exactly as near to God from any place as it is from any other place. No one is any further from or any closer to God in terms of distance than anyone else.

These are truths believed by every well-taught Christian. We need to think about them and pray over them until they start to glow within us.

"In the beginning God." Not matter, because matter doesn't cause itself. It needs a cause before it, and God is that Cause. Not law, because law is just a name for the path all creation follows. That path had to be planned, and the Planner is God. Not mind, because mind is also created and must have a Creator behind it. In the beginning God, the uncaused Cause of matter, mind, and law. That's where we must start.

Adam sinned and, in his panic, desperately tried to do the impossible: he tried to hide from God's Presence. David must have also had wild thoughts of trying to escape from the Presence, because he wrote, "Where can I go from your Spirit? Where can I flee from your presence?" Then he went on in one of his most beautiful psalms to celebrate the glory of God's presence everywhere. "If I go up to the heavens, you are there; if I make my bed in the depths, you are there. If I rise on the wings of the dawn, if I settle on the far side of the sea, even there your hand will guide me, your right hand will hold me fast." And he knew that God's being and God's seeing are the same, that the seeing Presence had been with him even before he was born, watching the mystery of unfolding life. Solomon exclaimed, "But will God really dwell on earth? The heavens, even the highest heaven, cannot contain you. How much less this temple I have built!" Paul assured the Athenians that "God is not far from any one of us. For in him we live and move and have our being."

If God is everywhere in space, if we can't go where He isn't, can't even imagine a place where He's not, why hasn't this Presence become the one fact everyone celebrates? Jacob, "in the howling wilderness," gave the answer. He saw a vision of God and cried out in wonder, "Surely the Lord is in this place, and I didn't know it." Jacob had never been outside God's all-present circle for even a moment. But he didn't know it. That was his problem, and it's ours. People don't know God is here. What a difference it would make if they knew.

The Presence and the awareness of the Presence aren't the same. One can happen without the other. God is here even when we're completely unaware. He's visible only when we're aware of His Presence. We must surrender to God's Spirit, because it's His job to show us the Father and the Son. If we work with Him in loving obedience, God will show Himself to us, and that showing will be the difference between a Christian in name only and a life shining with the light of His face.

Always, everywhere God is present, and always He tries to reveal Himself. To each person He wants to show not only that He is, but what He is. He didn't need to be convinced to show Himself to Moses. "And the Lord came down in the cloud and stood there with him and proclaimed his name, the Lord." He not only described His nature in words but showed Himself to Moses so that Moses' face shone with supernatural light. It will be a great moment for some of us when we start to believe that God's promise to reveal Himself is literally true: that He promised much, but no more than He plans to fulfill.

Our search for God succeeds just because He's always trying to show Himself to us. God revealing Himself to someone isn't God coming from far away to briefly visit that person's soul. Thinking of it that way is to misunderstand it all. God approaching the soul or the soul approaching God shouldn't be thought of in terms of physical distance at all. It's not about miles but about experience.

Talking about being near to or far from God is using language in the way we understand it in our normal human relationships. A man might say, "I feel my son is getting closer to me as he grows older," even though that son has lived with his father since birth and has never been away from home for more than a day or so in his whole life. What does the father mean? Obviously, he's talking about experience. He means the boy is getting to know him more closely and deeply, that the barriers of thought and feeling between them are disappearing, that father and son are becoming more closely united in mind and heart.

So when we sing, "Draw me nearer, nearer, blessed Lord," we're not thinking about physical nearness, but closeness of relationship. We're praying for greater awareness, for a clearer sense of God's Presence. We never need to shout across space to an absent God. He's closer than our own soul, nearer than our most secret thoughts.

Why do some people "find" God in a way others don't? Why does God show His Presence to some and let many others struggle in the dim light of imperfect Christian experience? Of course, God's will is the same for everyone. He has no favorites among His children. All He's ever done for any of His children He will do for all of them. The difference isn't with God but with us.

Pick randomly 20 great saints whose lives and stories are well known. They could be Bible characters or famous Christians from later times. You'll immediately notice that the saints weren't all alike. Sometimes the differences were so big they were obvious. For example, Moses was very different from Isaiah; Elijah was unlike David; John and Paul were quite different from each other, as were St. Francis and Luther, Finney and Thomas à Kempis. The differences are as wide as human life itself: differences in race, nationality, education, personality, habits, and personal qualities. Yet they all walked, each in their time, on a high road of spiritual living far above the common way.

Their differences must have been unimportant and, in God's eyes, not significant. In some vital quality, they must have been alike. What was it?

I suggest that the one vital quality they shared was spiritual receptivity. Something in them was open to heaven, something that pushed them towards God. Without trying to deeply analyze it, I'll simply say they had spiritual awareness and they worked to develop it until it became the biggest thing in their lives. They were different from the average person in that when they felt an inner longing, they did something about it. They developed a lifelong habit of spiritual response. They weren't disobedient to the heavenly vision. As David put it nicely, "When you said, 'Seek my face,' my heart said to you, 'Your face, Lord, I will seek.'"

As with everything good in human life, God is behind this receptivity. God's sovereignty is here, and is felt even by those who haven't particularly emphasized it in their theology. The devout Michelangelo admitted this in a sonnet:

My unassisted heart is barren clay,

That of its native self can nothing feed:

Of good and pious works Thou art the seed,

That quickens only where Thou sayest it may:

Unless Thou show to us Thine own true way

No man can find it: Father! Thou must lead.

These words are worth studying as the deep, serious testimony of a great Christian.

While it's important to recognize God working in us, I'd warn against thinking about it too much. That can lead to unproductive passivity. God won't hold us responsible for understanding the mysteries of election, predestination, and divine sovereignty. The best and safest way to deal with these truths is to look up to God and say with deep respect, "O Lord, You know." These things belong to the deep, mysterious depths of God's all-knowing nature. Prying into them might make theologians, but it won't make saints.

Receptivity isn't just one thing; it's a mix of several elements in the soul. It's an attraction to, a leaning towards, a sympathetic response to, a desire to have. From this, we can see that it can exist in degrees – we can have a little or more or less, depending on the person. It can grow with practice or be destroyed by neglect. It's not an overwhelming, irresistible force that comes on us like a seizure from above. It's a gift from God, yes, but one we must recognize and develop like any other gift if it's to fulfill its purpose.

Not seeing this has caused a very serious problem in modern evangelicalism. The idea of developing and practicing, so dear to the saints of old, now has no place in our overall religious picture. It's too slow, too ordinary. We now demand excitement and fast-paced, dramatic action. A generation of Christians raised with push buttons and automatic machines is impatient with slower, less direct ways of reaching their goals. We've been trying to apply machine-age methods to our relationship with God. We read our chapter, have our short devotions and rush away, hoping to make up for our deep inner poverty by going to another gospel meeting or listening to another thrilling story told by a religious adventurer just back from far away.

The sad results of this attitude are all around us. Shallow lives, empty religious philosophies, too much focus on fun in gospel meetings, glorifying people, trusting in outward religious signs, quasi-religious groups, sales methods, mistaking dynamic personality for the power of the Spirit: these and things like them are symptoms of a serious disease, a deep and serious sickness of the soul.

No one person is responsible for this great sickness that's upon us, and no Christian is completely free from blame. We've all contributed, directly or indirectly, to this sad state of affairs. We've been too blind to see, or too timid to speak out, or too self-satisfied to want anything better than the poor average diet that others seem satisfied with. Put differently, we've accepted each other's ideas, copied each other's lives, and made each other's experiences the model for our own. And for a generation, the trend has been downward. Now we've reached a low place of sand and burnt grass and, worst of all, we've made the Word of Truth fit our experience and accepted this low level as the very pasture of the blessed.

It will take a determined heart and more than a little courage to break free from the grip of our times and return to Biblical ways. But it can be done. Every now and then in the past, Christians have had to do it. History has recorded several large-scale returns led by men like St. Francis, Martin Luther, and George Fox. Unfortunately, there doesn't seem to be a Luther or Fox on the horizon right now. Whether or not we can expect another such return before Christ comes is a question Christians don't fully agree on, but that's not too important to us now.

I don't claim to know what God in His power might still do on a world scale. But I believe I do know and can tell others what He will do for the ordinary person who sincerely seeks Him. Let anyone turn to God earnestly, let them start to practice godliness, let them try to develop their ability to receive spiritual things through trust, obedience, and humility, and the results will be better than anything they might have hoped for in their weaker days.

Anyone who, through repentance and a sincere return to God, breaks out of the mold they've been stuck in, and goes to the Bible itself for their spiritual standards, will be delighted with what they find there.

Let's say it again: God's presence everywhere is a fact. God is here. The whole universe is alive with His life. And He's not a strange or foreign God, but the familiar Father of our Lord Jesus Christ whose love has, for thousands of years, embraced sinful humanity. And He's always trying to get our attention, to reveal Himself to us, to communicate with us. We have the ability within us to know Him if we'll just respond to His attempts to reach us. (And this is what we call pursuing God!) We'll know Him more and more as we become better at receiving Him through faith, love, and practice.

O God and Father, I'm sorry for being so focused on visible things. The world has been too much with me. You've been here and I didn't know it. I've been blind to Your Presence. Open my eyes so I can see You in and around me. For Christ's sake, Amen.

Study Guide

> "Wherever we are, God is here. There is no place, there can be no place, where He is not."

How does the concept of God's universal presence challenge or comfort you? Are there places where you find it harder to believe God is present?

The author states, "God is here." How might fully embracing this truth change your daily life and interactions?

Examine 1 Kings 8:27-30 (Solomon's prayer at the temple dedication). How does Solomon grapple with the concept of God's universal presence?

> "They were different from the average person in that when they felt an inner longing, they did something about it."

Reflect on a time when you strongly felt God's presence. What factors contributed to your awareness of Him in that moment?

Examine what enhances or diminishes your ability to sense God's presence. Create a plan to cultivate greater receptivity this week.

How do you reconcile the idea of God's constant presence with times when He feels distant?

Study Jeremiah 23:23-24. How does God describe His own presence? What implications does this have for our understanding of Him?

Set hourly reminders on your phone. Each time it goes off, pause to acknowledge God's presence right where you are.

Personal Reflection and Journal

Use this space to write your responses, insights, and experiences as you work through this study. Consider the following prompts:

- In what areas of my life do I need to invite God's presence more consciously?

- What challenges am I facing to live in awareness of God's omnipresence?

- How is embracing God's universal presence changing my perspective on daily life?

"Lord, open my eyes to see Your presence in every moment and every place. Help me to live in constant awareness of You. Increase my spiritual receptivity. Remove any barriers that prevent me from sensing Your presence fully. Guide me into a deeper understanding of God's omnipresence. Help me to live in light of this truth."

The Speaking Voice

In the beginning was the Word, and the Word was with God, and the Word was God. John 1:1

An intelligent, ordinary person, not taught Christian truths, reading this text, might think John meant to say that it's God's nature to speak, to share His thoughts with others. And they'd be right. A word is how thoughts are expressed, and using this term for the Eternal Son makes us think that expressing Himself is part of who God is, that God is always trying to communicate Himself to His creation. The whole Bible supports this idea. God is speaking. Not God spoke, but God is speaking. By His nature, He's always communicating. He fills the world with His speaking Voice.

One of the big realities we deal with is God's Voice in His world. The shortest and only satisfying explanation of how the world began is this: "He spoke and it happened." The reason for natural law is God's living Voice present in His creation. And this word of God that brought all worlds into being doesn't mean the Bible, because it's not a written or printed word at all, but God's will spoken into the structure of all things. This word of God is God's breath filling the world with living potential. God's Voice is the strongest force in nature, in fact the only force in nature, because all energy exists only because the power-filled Word is being spoken.

The Bible is God's written word, and because it's written, it's limited by ink, paper, and leather. But God's Voice is alive and free as God Himself is free. "The words I speak to you are spirit and life." The life is in the spoken words. God's word in the Bible can only have power because it matches God's word in the universe. It's the present Voice that makes the written Word all-powerful. Otherwise, it would just lie asleep inside a book.

We have a simple, primitive view of things when we think of God at creation physically touching things, shaping and building like a carpenter. The Bible teaches differently: "By the word of the Lord the heavens were made, their starry host by the breath of his mouth... For he spoke, and it came to be; he commanded, and it stood firm." "By faith, we understand that the universe was formed at God's command." Again, we must remember God isn't talking about His written Word here, but His speaking Voice. He means His world-filling Voice, the Voice that came before the Bible by countless centuries, the Voice that hasn't been silent since creation began, but is still sounding throughout the whole universe.

God's Word is alive and powerful. In the beginning, He spoke to nothing, and it became something. Chaos heard it and became order, darkness heard it and became light. "And God said—and it was so." These paired phrases, as cause and effect, appear throughout the Genesis creation story. The "said" accounts for the "so". The "so" is the "said" put into the ongoing present.

That God is here and that He is speaking—these truths are behind all other Bible truths; without them there could be no revelation at all. God didn't write a book and send it by messenger to be read from afar by unaided minds. He spoke a Book and lives in His spoken words, constantly speaking His words and making their power last through the years. God breathed on clay and it became a man; He breathes on men and they become clay. "Return, you children of men" was the word spoken at the Fall by which God decreed every man's death, and He hasn't needed to speak any more words. The sad parade of humanity across the earth from birth to death proves that His original Word was enough.

We haven't paid enough attention to that deep saying in John's book: "The true light that gives light to everyone was coming into the world." No matter how we arrange the punctuation, the truth remains: God's Word affects all people's hearts like light in the soul. In everyone's heart, the light shines, the Word sounds, and there's no escaping them. This would have to be true if God is alive and in His world. And John says it is. Even people who've never heard of the Bible have still been preached to clearly enough to remove any excuse from their hearts forever. "They show that the requirements of the law are written on their hearts, their consciences also bearing witness, and their thoughts sometimes accusing them and at other times even defending them." "For since the creation of the world God's invisible qualities—his eternal power and divine nature—have been clearly seen, being understood from what has been made, so that people are without excuse."

This universal Voice of God was often called Wisdom by the ancient Hebrews. They said it was everywhere, sounding and searching throughout the earth, looking for some response from people. The eighth chapter of Proverbs begins, "Does not wisdom call out? Does not understanding raise her voice?" The writer then describes wisdom as a beautiful woman standing "on the heights along the way, where the paths meet." She calls out from everywhere so no one can miss hearing her. "To you, O people, I call out; I raise my voice to all mankind." Then she asks the simple and foolish to listen to her words. It's a spiritual response that this Wisdom of God is asking for, a response she's always sought but rarely gets. The tragedy is that our eternal well-being depends on our hearing, and we've trained our ears not to hear.

This universal Voice has always sounded, and it has often troubled people even when they didn't understand why they were afraid. Could it be that this Voice, spreading like a living mist on people's hearts, has been the unknown cause of the troubled conscience and longing for immortality that millions have admitted to since history began? We shouldn't be afraid to face this. The speaking Voice is real. How people have reacted to it is for anyone to see.

When God spoke from heaven to Jesus, self-centered people who heard it explained it away: they said, "It thundered." This habit of explaining the Voice by natural causes is at the very heart of modern science. In the living, breathing universe, there's a mysterious Something, too wonderful, too awesome for any mind to understand. The believer doesn't claim to understand. He falls to his knees and whispers, "God." The earthly person kneels too, but not to worship. He kneels to examine, to search, to find the cause and the how of things. Right now, we happen to be living in a non-religious age. Our thinking habits are those of the scientist, not the worshipper. We're more likely to explain than to adore. "It thundered," we say, and go on our earthly way. But still, the Voice sounds and searches. The order and life of the world depend on that Voice, but people are mostly too busy or too stubborn to pay attention.

Each of us has had experiences we can't explain: a sudden feeling of loneliness, or wonder or awe at the vastness of the universe. Or we've had a brief flash of light, as if from another sun, giving us a quick assurance that we're from another world, that our origins are divine. What we saw, felt, or heard might have gone against everything we learned in school and differed greatly from all our previous beliefs and opinions. We had to set aside our learned doubts while, for a moment, the clouds parted and we saw and heard for ourselves. However we explain such things, I think we're not being fair to the facts until we at least consider that these experiences might come from God's Presence in the world and His constant effort to communicate with humanity. Let's not dismiss this idea too quickly.

I personally believe (and I won't mind if no one agrees) that every good and beautiful thing humans have produced in the world has come from their flawed and sin-blocked response to the creative Voice sounding over the earth. The moral philosophers who dreamed of high virtue, the religious thinkers who pondered God and immortality, the poets and artists who created lasting beauty from ordinary things: how can we explain them? It's not enough to just say, "It was genius." What then is genius? Could it be that a genius is someone haunted by the speaking Voice, working and striving like someone possessed to achieve goals they only vaguely understand? The fact that great people might have missed God in their work, or even spoken or written against God, doesn't disprove my idea. God's saving revelation in the Bible is necessary for saving faith and peace with God. Faith in a risen Savior is necessary if vague stirrings toward immortality are to bring us to restful and satisfying communion with God. To me, this explains all that's best outside of Christ. But you can be a good Christian and not agree with me.

God's Voice is friendly. No one needs to fear listening to it unless they've already decided to resist it. Jesus' blood has covered not just humanity but all creation too. "And through him to reconcile to himself all things, whether things on earth or things in heaven, by making peace through his blood, shed on the cross." We can safely preach about a friendly Heaven. The heavens and the earth are filled with the goodwill of the One who appeared in the burning bush. The perfect blood of atonement secures this forever.

Anyone who will listen will hear Heaven speaking. This isn't a time when people take kindly to being told to listen, because listening isn't part of popular religion today. We're at the opposite end from there. Religion has accepted the terrible mistake that noise, size, activity, and show make a person dear to God. But we can take heart. To people caught in the storm of the last great conflict, God says, "Be still, and know that I am God," and He still says it, as if to tell us that our strength and safety lie not in noise but in silence.

It's important that we get quiet to wait on God. It's best to be alone, preferably with our Bible open before us. Then, if we choose, we can draw near to God and start to hear Him speak to our hearts. For most people, I think it will go something like this: First, a sound like someone walking in a garden. Then a voice, clearer but still not distinct. Then the wonderful moment when the Spirit starts to illuminate the Scriptures, and what was only a sound, or at best a voice, now becomes clear words, warm and personal, like the words of a close friend. Then will come life and light, and best of all, the ability to see, rest in, and embrace Jesus Christ as Savior, Lord, and Everything.

The Bible won't be a living Book to us until we're convinced that God speaks in His universe. To jump from a dead, impersonal world to a dog-matic Bible is too much for most people. They might admit they should accept the Bible as God's Word, and they might try to think of it that way, but they find it impossible to believe the words on the page are actually for them. A person might say, "These words are addressed to me," but in their heart not feel and know that they are. They're split inside. They try to think of God as silent everywhere else and only speaking in a book.

I believe much of our religious unbelief comes from a wrong idea of and feeling for the Scriptures. We think of a silent God who suddenly started speaking in a book and when the book was finished, went back to silence forever. Now we read the book as a record of what God said when He was briefly in a speaking mood. With ideas like that, how can we believe? The truth is, God is not silent, has never been silent. It's God's nature to speak. The second Person of the Trinity is called the Word. The Bible is the inevitable result of God's continuous speech. It's the perfect declaration of His mind for us put into our familiar human words.

I think a new world will emerge from religious confusion when we approach our Bible with the idea that it's not only a book that was once spoken, but a book that is now speaking. The prophets often said, "This is what the Lord says." They meant their listeners to understand that God's speaking is ongoing. We can use the past tense to say that at a certain time a certain word of God was spoken, but a word of God once spoken continues to be spoken, like a child once born continues to be alive, or a world once created continues to exist. And those are imperfect examples, because children die and worlds burn out, but God's Word lasts forever.

If you want to follow on to know the Lord, come right away to the open Bible expecting it to speak to you. Don't come thinking it's a thing you can push around as you like. It's more than a thing, it's a voice, a word, the very Word of the living God.

Lord, teach me to listen. The world is noisy and my ears are tired from the thousand harsh sounds that constantly hit them. Give me the spirit of the boy Samuel when he said to You, "Speak, for your servant is listening." Let me hear You speaking in my heart. Let me get used to the sound of Your Voice, so its tones will be familiar when earth's sounds fade away and the only sound will be the music of Your speaking Voice. Amen.

Study Guide

> "God is speaking. Not God spoke, but God is speaking. By His nature, He's always communicating. He fills the world with His speaking Voice."

How does the concept of God continually speaking, rather than having spoken in the past, change your perspective on His communication with us?

How might the concept of God's continual speaking impact your approach to prayer and listening to God?

Study 1 Samuel 3:1-10. What can we learn about hearing God's voice from Samuel's experience?

> "It is the nature of God to speak. The second Person of the Holy Trinity is called the Word."

Choose a short passage of Scripture to meditate on. As you read, ask God to speak to you through His written Word. Record any insights you gain.

Read Hebrews 1:1-3. How does this passage describe God's communication with humanity?

Reflect on a time when you felt you heard God's voice. What was that experience like? How did you know it was God speaking?

Examine John 10:1-18. How does Jesus describe His own voice and His sheep's response to it? What implications does this have for us?

"It's important that we get quiet to wait on God. It's best to be alone, preferably with our Bible open before us. Then, if we choose, we can draw near to God and start to hear Him speak to our hearts."

Spend 15 minutes a day this week in silent prayer and Bible reading. Focus on listening for God's voice rather than speaking. Journal your thoughts.

Personal Reflection and Journal

Use this space to write your responses, insights, and experiences as you work through this study. Consider the following prompts:

- In what ways am I learning to recognize and respond to God's speaking Voice?

- What challenges am I facing in hearing God speak in my daily life?

- How is the concept of God's continual speaking impacting my relationship with Him?

"Lord, open my ears to hear Your speaking Voice. Help me recognize it amidst the noise of the world. I want to experience the power of Your Voice in my life. Speak to me and transform me by Your Word. Guide me into all truth as I seek to hear and obey God's Voice. Give me discernment to distinguish Your voice from others."

The Gaze of the Soul

Looking unto Jesus the author and finisher of our faith. Heb. 12:2

Let's think about our average, intelligent person from chapter six coming to read the Bible for the first time. He approaches the Bible without any prior knowledge of what's in it. He has no bias; he's not trying to prove or defend anything.

This person won't have read for long before his mind starts to notice certain truths standing out from the page. These are the spiritual principles behind the story of God's dealings with people, woven into the writings of holy men as they "were moved by the Holy Spirit." As he reads on, he might want to number these truths as they become clear to him and make a short summary under each number. These summaries will be the beliefs of his Biblical creed. Further reading won't change these points, except to expand and strengthen them. Our reader is discovering what the Bible actually teaches.

High on the list of things the Bible teaches will be the idea of faith. The importance the Bible gives to faith will be too clear for him to miss. He'll likely conclude: Faith is crucial in the life of the soul. Without faith, it's impossible to please God. Faith will get me anything, take me anywhere in God's Kingdom, but without faith there can be no approach to God, no forgiveness, no deliverance, no salvation, no communion, no spiritual life at all.

By the time our friend reaches the eleventh chapter of Hebrews, the eloquent praise of faith there won't seem strange to him. He'll have read Paul's strong defense of faith in his letters to the Romans and Galatians. Later, if he studies church history, he'll understand the amazing power in the Reformers' teachings as they showed the central place of faith in Christianity.

Now if faith is so vital, if it's an essential must in our pursuit of God, it's natural that we should be deeply concerned about whether we have this precious gift. And given how our minds work, it's inevitable that sooner or later we'd start asking about the nature of faith. What is faith? This question would be close to asking, Do I have faith? and would demand an answer if one could be found.

Almost everyone who preaches or writes about faith says much the same things about it. They tell us it's believing a promise, taking God at His word, considering the Bible to be true and acting on it. The rest of the book or sermon is usually filled with stories of people whose prayers were answered because of their faith. These answers are mostly direct gifts of a practical and temporary nature like health, money, physical protection, or success in business. Or if the teacher is more philosophical, he might take another approach and confuse us with complex ideas or overwhelm us with psychological terms as he defines and redefines faith, making it thinner and thinner until it disappears into wispy shavings. When he's finished, we get up disappointed and leave the same way we came in. Surely there must be something better than this.

The Bible doesn't really try to define faith. Apart from a short fourteen-word definition in Hebrews 11:1, I don't know of any Biblical definition. Even there, faith is defined by what it does, not by what it is. It assumes faith is present and shows what it results in, rather than what it is. We'd be wise to go just that far and try to go no further. We're told where it comes from and how: "Faith is a gift of God," and "Faith comes from hearing the message, and the message is heard through the word about Christ." This much is clear, and to rephrase Thomas à Kempis, "I'd rather practice faith than know its definition."

From here on, when I say "faith is" in this chapter, I mean what faith looks like in action, as practiced by a believing person. We're dropping the idea of definition and thinking about faith as it's experienced in action. Our thoughts will be practical, not theoretical.

In a dramatic story in Numbers, we see faith in action. Israel got discouraged and spoke against God, so God sent poisonous snakes among them. "They bit the people, and many Israelites died." Then Moses prayed for them and God heard and gave them a cure for the snake bites. He told Moses to make a bronze snake and put it on a pole where everyone could see it, "and anyone who is bitten can look at it and live." Moses obeyed, "and when anyone was bitten by a snake and looked at the bronze snake, they lived."

In the New Testament, Jesus Himself explains this important bit of history. He's telling His listeners how they can be saved. He says it's by believing. Then to make it clear, He refers to this incident in Numbers. "Just as Moses lifted up the snake in the wilderness, so the Son of Man must be lifted up, that everyone who believes may have eternal life in him."

Our average reader would make an important discovery here. He'd notice that "look" and "believe" mean the same thing. "Looking" at the Old Testament snake is the same as "believing" in the New Testament Christ. That is, looking and believing are the same thing. And he'd understand that while Israel looked with their physical eyes, believing is done with the heart. I think he'd conclude that faith is the soul's gaze upon a saving God.

When he saw this, he'd remember passages he'd read before, and their meaning would become clear to him. "Those who look to him are radiant; their faces are never covered with shame." "I lift up my eyes to you, to you who sit enthroned in heaven. As the eyes of slaves look to the hand of their master, as the eyes of a female slave look to the hand of her mistress, so our eyes look to the Lord our God, till he shows us his mercy." Here, the person seeking mercy looks straight at the God of mercy and doesn't look away until mercy is given. And Jesus Himself always looked to God. "Looking up to heaven, he gave thanks and broke the loaves." In fact, Jesus taught that He did His works by always keeping His inner eyes on His Father. His power came from His constant focus on God.

The whole Bible agrees with these few texts we've quoted. It's summed up for us in Hebrews when we're told to run life's race "fixing our eyes on Jesus, the pioneer and perfecter of faith." From all this, we learn that faith isn't a one-time act, but a continuous gaze of the heart at the Triune God.

Believing, then, is directing the heart's attention to Jesus. It's lifting the mind to "look at the Lamb of God," and keeping that focus for the rest of our lives. At first this might be hard, but it gets easier as we steadily look at His wonderful Person, quietly and without strain. Distractions may get in the way, but once the heart is committed to Him, after each brief distraction, the attention will return and rest on Him like a wandering bird coming back to its window.

I want to emphasize this one commitment, this one big willful act that sets the heart's intention to gaze forever on Jesus. God takes this intention as our choice and makes allowances for the thousand distractions that bother us in this evil world. He knows we've set our hearts toward Jesus, and we can know it too, and take comfort in knowing that a habit of the soul is forming which will eventually become a kind of spiritual reflex needing no more conscious effort from us.

Faith is the least self-focused of the virtues. By its nature, it's hardly aware of its own existence. Like the eye which sees everything in front of it and never sees itself, faith is focused on the Object it rests on and pays no attention to itself at all. While we're looking at God, we don't see ourselves—what a blessing. The person who has struggled to purify himself and has only had repeated failures will feel real relief when he stops tinkering with his soul and looks away to the perfect One. While he looks at Christ, the very things he's been trying so long to do will be happening within him. It will be God working in him to will and to act.

Faith itself isn't a praiseworthy act; the merit is in the One it's directed towards. Faith is redirecting our sight, getting our own vision out of focus and bringing God into focus. Sin has twisted our vision inward and made it self-centered. Unbelief has put self where God should be, and is dangerously close to Lucifer's sin of saying, "I will set my throne above God's throne." Faith looks out instead of in, and the whole life falls into place.

All this might seem too simple. But we don't apologize for it. To those who would try to climb to heaven for help or go down to hell, God says, "The word is near you; it is in your mouth and in your heart." The word encourages us to look up to the Lord and the blessed work of faith begins.

When we look inwardly at God, we're sure to meet friendly eyes looking back at us, because it's written that the eyes of the Lord range throughout the earth. The sweet language of experience is "You are the God who sees me." When the soul's eyes looking out meet God's eyes looking in, heaven has begun right here on earth.

"When all my effort is turned toward You because all Your effort is turned toward me; when I look at You alone with all my attention, never turning aside my mind's eyes, because You constantly watch over me; when I direct my love toward You alone because You, who are Love itself, have turned toward me alone. And what, Lord, is my life, except that embrace where Your delightful sweetness so lovingly enfolds me?" So wrote Nicholas of Cusa four hundred years ago.

I'd like to say more about this old man of God. He's not well known today among Christian believers, and among current Fundamentalists he's not known at all. I think we could gain a lot from getting to know men of his spiritual type and the school of Christian thought they represent. Christian literature, to be accepted and approved by today's evangelical leaders, must follow very closely the same line of thought, a kind of "party line" that it's hardly safe to depart from. Half a century of this in America has made us smug and content. We imitate each other slavishly and our hardest efforts are spent trying to say the same thing everyone around us is saying—and yet to find an excuse for saying it, some small safe variation on the approved theme or, if nothing else, at least a new illustration.

Nicholas was a true follower of Christ, a lover of the Lord, glowing in his devotion to Jesus. His theology was correct, but sweet and fragrant as everything about Jesus should be. His idea of eternal life, for example, is beautiful in itself and, if I'm not mistaken, is closer in spirit to John 17:3 than what's common among us today. Eternal life, says Nicholas, is "nothing other than that blessed gaze with which You never stop looking at me, even into the secret places of my soul. With You, to look is to give life; it's to constantly share the sweetest love of You; it's to inflame me to love You by sharing love; it's to feed me by inflaming, and by feeding to spark my yearning, and by sparking to make me drink the dew of joy, and by drinking to pour into me a fountain of life, and by pouring to make it grow and last."

Now, if faith is the heart's gaze at God, and if this gaze is just lifting the inner eyes to meet God's all-seeing eyes, then it follows that it's one of the easiest things possible to do. It would be like God to make the most vital thing easy and put it within reach of the weakest and poorest of us.

We can draw several conclusions from all this. The simplicity of it, for instance. Since believing is looking, it can be done without special equipment or religious tools. God has made sure that the one life-and-death essential can never depend on chance. Equipment can break or get lost, water can leak, records can burn, the minister can be late or the church can burn down. All these are outside the soul and can fail or break: but looking is from the heart and can be done successfully by anyone standing up or kneeling down or lying in their last moments a thousand miles from any church.

Since believing is looking, it can be done anytime. No time is better than another for this sweetest of all acts. God never made salvation depend on new moons or holy days or sabbaths. A person isn't closer to Christ on Easter Sunday than they are on, say, Saturday, August 3, or Monday, October 4. As long as Christ sits on the mediator's throne, every day is a good day and all days are days of salvation.

Place doesn't matter either in this blessed work of believing God. Lift your heart and let it rest on Jesus and you're instantly in a sanctuary even if it's a train bed or a factory or a kitchen. You can see God from anywhere if your mind is set to love and obey Him.

Now, someone might ask, "Isn't this just for special people like monks or ministers who have more time for quiet thinking? I'm a busy worker with little time alone." I'm happy to say that the life I describe is for all of God's children, no matter what their job. In fact, many hardworking people happily practice this every day, and it's within everyone's reach.

Many have found this secret and, without thinking much about what's happening inside them, constantly practice this habit of inwardly looking at God. They know that something in their hearts sees God. Even when they have to focus on earthly matters, there's a secret communion always going on inside them. As soon as they can free their attention from necessary work, it flies back to God. Many Christians have said this, so many that I feel like I'm quoting someone, though I can't say who or how many.

I don't want to give the impression that the usual ways of growing spiritually aren't valuable. They certainly are. Every Christian should pray privately. Long periods of thinking about the Bible will purify our gaze and direct it; going to church will broaden our outlook and increase our love for others. Service, work, and activity are all good and every Christian should do them. But underneath all these things, giving them meaning, will be the inner habit of looking at God. A new set of eyes (so to speak) will develop in us, letting us look at God while our outer eyes see the scenes of this passing world.

Someone might worry that we're making private religion too important, that the "us" of the New Testament is being replaced by a selfish "I." Have you ever thought that one hundred pianos all tuned to the same fork are automatically in tune with each other? They're in harmony by being tuned, not to each other, but to another standard that each one must individually match. In the same way, one hundred worshippers gathered together, each looking to Christ, are closer to each other in heart than they could possibly be if they became "unity" conscious and turned their eyes away from God to try for closer fellowship. Social religion is perfected when private religion is purified. The body becomes stronger as its members become healthier. The whole Church of God gains when its members start to seek a better and higher life.

All of this assumes true repentance and a full commitment of life to God. I hardly need to mention this, because only people who have made such a commitment will have read this far.

When the habit of inwardly looking towards God becomes fixed in us, we'll be brought to a new level of spiritual life more in line with God's promises and the mood of the New Testament. The Triune God will be our home even while we walk the simple path of duty here among people. We will have found life's highest good indeed. "There is the source of all delights that can be desired; not only can nothing better be thought of by men and angels, but nothing better can exist in any way of being! For it is the absolute maximum of every rational desire, than which nothing greater can be."

O Lord, I have heard a good word inviting me to look away to You and be satisfied. My heart longs to respond, but sin has clouded my vision till I see You only dimly. Please cleanse me in Your own precious blood, and make me inwardly pure, so that I may with clear eyes gaze upon You all the days of my earthly journey. Then I shall be ready to see You in full splendor on the day when You will appear to be glorified in Your saints and admired in all those who believe. Amen.

Study Guide

The author describes faith as "the gaze of a soul upon a saving God." How does this definition compare with your previous understanding of faith?

Read Numbers 21:4-9 and John 3:14-15. How does Jesus use this Old Testament story to illustrate faith? How does it relate to the "gaze of the soul"?

> "The person who has struggled to purify himself and has only had repeated failures will feel real relief when he stops tinkering with his soul and looks away to the perfect One."

Reflect on your approach to personal holiness. Are you more prone to self-effort or to "looking away to the perfect One"?

> "I want to emphasize this one commitment, this one big willful act that sets the heart's intention to gaze forever on Jesus."

What challenges might you face in maintaining a constant focus on Jesus?

Study 2 Corinthians 3:18. How does Paul describe the transformative power of beholding the Lord?

"Faith is the least self-focused of the virtues. By its nature, it's hardly aware of its own existence. Like the eye which sees everything in front of it and never sees itself, faith is focused on the Object it rests on and pays no attention to itself at all."

How does the concept of faith being "hardly aware of its own existence" challenge or affirm your experience of faith?

In what ways have you found yourself becoming self-conscious about your faith? How might the ideas in this chapter help address that?

Take notice when your attention shifts to your spiritual performance. Practice redirecting your focus to Jesus instead.

Personal Reflection and Journal

Use this space to write your responses, insights, and experiences as you work through this study. Consider the following prompts:

- How is my understanding of faith changing through this study of "the gaze of the soul"?

- In what ways am I learning to maintain a more constant focus on Jesus?

- What challenges am I facing in shifting my attention from self-awareness to Christ-awareness in my faith?

"Lord Jesus, help me to fix my gaze upon You. Let my faith be a constant beholding of Your beauty and grace. Free me from self-consciousness in my faith. Let my attention be fully on You rather than on my own spiritual achievements. Teach me to maintain a steady gaze on Jesus amidst life's distractions and challenges."

Restoring the Creator-creature Relation

Be exalted, O God, above the heavens; Let Your glory be above all the earth.
Ps. 57:5

It's obvious that order in nature depends on right relationships; to achieve harmony, each thing must be in its proper position relative to everything else. In human life, it's the same.

I've hinted before that the cause of all our human troubles is a deep moral disorder, a disruption in our relationship with God and each other. Whatever else the Fall might have been, it was certainly a big change in man's relationship to his Creator. He took on a different attitude toward God, and by doing so, ruined the proper Creator-creature relationship in which, without realizing it, his true happiness lay. Basically, salvation is fixing the right relationship between man and his Creator, bringing the Creator-creature relationship back to normal.

A good spiritual life will start with a complete change in the relationship between God and the sinner; not just a legal change, but a conscious and felt change affecting the sinner's whole nature. Jesus' sacrifice makes such a change legally possible, and the Holy Spirit's work makes it emotionally satisfying. The story of the prodigal son perfectly shows this last part. He had caused himself a world of trouble by leaving his proper position as his father's son. At its core, his restoration was simply re-establishing the father-son relationship that had existed since his birth and had been temporarily changed by his sinful rebellion. This story doesn't focus on the legal aspects of redemption, but it beautifully shows the experiential aspects of salvation.

In figuring out relationships, we have to start somewhere. There must be a fixed center against which everything else is measured, where the law of relativity doesn't apply and we can say "IS" without making any exceptions. Such a center is God. When God wanted to make His Name known to mankind, He couldn't find a better word than "I AM." When He speaks in the first person He says, "I AM"; when we speak of Him we say, "He is"; when we speak to Him we say, "You are." Everyone and everything else measures from that fixed point. "I am who I am," says God, "I do not change."

Just as a sailor finds his position at sea by measuring the sun's position, we can get our moral bearings by looking at God. We must start with God. We are right when and only when we stand in the right position relative to God, and we are wrong as far and as long as we stand in any other position.

Much of our difficulty as seeking Christians comes from our unwillingness to take God as He is and adjust our lives accordingly. We insist on trying to change Him and bring Him closer to our own image. Our human nature complains against the strictness of God's uncompromising judgment and begs like Agag for a little mercy, a little allowance for its worldly ways. It's no use. We can only get a right start by accepting God as He is and learning to love Him for what He is. As we get to know Him better, we'll find it a source of indescribable joy that God is exactly what He is. Some of our most joyful moments will be those we spend in respectful admiration of God. In those holy moments, the very thought of God changing will be too painful to bear.

So let's start with God. Behind all, above all, before all is God; first in order, highest in rank and position, supreme in dignity and honor. As the self-existing One, He gave being to all things, and all things exist from Him and for Him. "You are worthy, our Lord and God, to receive glory and honor and power, for you created all things, and by your will they were created and have their being."

Every soul belongs to God and exists by His choice. Given who and what God is, and who and what we are, the only thinkable relationship between us is one of complete lordship on His part and total submission on ours. We owe Him every honor we can give. Our eternal sorrow lies in giving Him anything less.

Pursuing God will involve bringing our whole personality into line with His. And this not just legally, but actually. I'm not talking about the act of being made right with God through faith in Christ. I mean voluntarily putting God in His proper place over us and willingly surrendering our whole being to the position of worshipful submission that the Creator-creature situation makes right.

The moment we decide we're going to exalt God above all, we step out of the world's parade. We'll find ourselves out of step with the world's ways, and more so as we progress on the holy path. We'll gain a new viewpoint; a new and different way of thinking will form in us; a new power will start to surprise us by its rising up and flowing out.

Our break with the world will directly result from our changed relationship with God. The world of fallen people doesn't honor God. Millions call themselves by His Name, true, and pay some token respect to Him, but a simple test will show how little He's really honored among them. Put the average person to the test on who is above, and their true position will be exposed. Force them to choose between God and money, God and people, God and personal ambition, God and self, God and human love, and God will come second every time. Those other things will be put above Him. However much the person may protest, the proof is in the choices they make day after day throughout their life.

"Be exalted" is the language of victorious spiritual experience. It's a small key to unlock the door to great treasures of grace. It's central in God's life in the soul. Let the seeking person reach a point where life and words join to say constantly "Be exalted," and a thousand minor problems will be solved at once. Their Christian life stops being the complicated thing it was before and becomes very simple. By using their will, they've set their course, and on that course they'll stay as if guided by an automatic pilot. If blown off course for a moment by some opposing wind, they'll surely return as if by a secret leaning of the soul. The hidden movements of the Spirit are working in their favor, and "the stars in their courses" fight for them. They've met their life problem at its center, and everything else must follow.

Let no one think they'll lose any human dignity by this voluntary sell-out of their all to God. This doesn't lower them as a person; rather, they find their right place of high honor as one made in their Creator's image. Their deep disgrace lay in their moral disorder, their unnatural taking of God's place. Their honor will be proved by giving back that stolen throne. In exalting God above all, they find their own highest honor upheld.

Anyone who might feel reluctant to give up their will to another's should remember Jesus' words, "Whoever commits sin is a slave to sin." We must necessarily be a servant to someone, either to God or to sin. The sinner prides themselves on their independence, completely overlooking that they're the weak slave of the sins that control them. The person who surrenders to Christ exchanges a cruel slave driver for a kind and gentle Master whose yoke is easy and whose burden is light.

Made as we were in God's image, we naturally find it easy to take God again as our All. God was our original home and our hearts can't help but feel at home when they enter again that ancient and beautiful place.

I hope it's clear that there's a logic behind God's claim to be first. That place is His by every right in earth or heaven. While we take for ourselves the place that is His, our whole lives are out of order. Nothing will or can restore order until our hearts make the big decision: God shall be exalted above all.

"Those who honor me I will honor," God once said to a priest of Israel, and that ancient law of the Kingdom stands unchanged today despite the passing of time or changes in how God deals with people. The whole Bible and every page of history proclaim that this law continues. "If anyone serves me, my Father will honor him," said our Lord Jesus, connecting the old with the new and showing the essential unity of His ways with people.

Sometimes the best way to see something is to look at its opposite. Eli and his sons are put in the priesthood with the condition that they honor God in their lives and service. They fail to do this, and God sends Samuel to announce the consequences. Unknown to Eli, this law of mutual honor has been secretly working all along, and now it's time for judgment. Hophni and Phinehas, the corrupt priests, die in battle, Hophni's wife dies in childbirth, Israel runs from her enemies, the ark of God is captured by the Philistines, and old Eli falls backward and dies of a broken neck. This total tragedy followed Eli's failure to honor God.

Now compare this with almost any Bible character who honestly tried to glorify God in their earthly life. See how God overlooked weaknesses and failures as He poured out grace and blessing on His servants. Whether it's Abraham, Jacob, David, Daniel, Elijah, or anyone else; honor followed honor like harvest follows seed. The person of God set their heart to exalt

God above all; God accepted their intention as fact and acted accordingly. Not perfection, but holy intention made the difference.

In our Lord Jesus Christ, this law was seen in simple perfection. In His humble humanity, He humbled Himself and gladly gave all glory to His Father in heaven. He didn't seek His own honor, but the honor of God who sent Him. "If I honor myself," He said once, "my honor is nothing; it is my Father who honors me." The proud Pharisees had strayed so far from this law that they couldn't understand someone who honored God at his own expense. "I honor my Father," Jesus said to them, "and you dishonor me."

Another saying of Jesus, a very troubling one, was put as a question: "How can you believe if you accept praise from one another, yet make no effort to obtain the praise that comes from the only God?" If I understand this right, Christ taught the alarming idea that wanting honor from people made belief impossible. Is this sin at the root of religious unbelief? Could it be that those "intellectual difficulties" people blame for not being able to believe are just smoke screens hiding the real cause? Was it this greedy desire for honor from people that turned men into Pharisees and Pharisees into God-killers? Is this the secret behind religious self-righteousness and empty worship? I think it might be. The whole course of life is upset by failing to put God where He belongs. We exalt ourselves instead of God and the curse follows.

In our desire for God, let's always remember that God also has desire, and His desire is for people, especially those who make the once-for-all decision to exalt Him above all. Such people are more precious to God than all the treasures of earth or sea. In them, God finds a stage where He can show His great kindness toward us in Christ Jesus. With them, God can walk freely, toward them He can act like the God He is.

In saying this, I have one fear: that I might convince the mind before God can win the heart. This God-above-all position isn't easy to take. The mind might approve it while the will doesn't agree to put it into effect. While the imagination races ahead to honor God, the will might lag behind and the person never realize how divided their heart is. The whole person must make the decision before the heart can feel any real satisfaction. God wants all of us, and He won't rest until He gets all of us. No part of us will do.

Let's pray about this in detail, throwing ourselves at God's feet and meaning everything we say. No one who prays like this sincerely needs to wait long for signs of God's acceptance. God will reveal His glory to His servant's eyes, and He will put all His treasures at their disposal because He knows His honor is safe in such dedicated hands.

O God, be exalted over my possessions. Nothing of earth's treasures shall seem dear to me if only You are glorified in my life. Be exalted over my friendships. I am determined that You shall be above all, even if I must stand deserted and alone in the world. Be exalted above my comforts. Even if it means losing bodily comforts and carrying heavy burdens, I shall keep my promise made today before You. Be exalted over my reputation. Make me eager to please You even if, as a result, I must sink into obscurity and my name be forgotten like a dream. Rise, O Lord, into Your proper place of honor, above my ambitions, above my likes and dislikes, above my family, my health, and even my life itself. Let me decrease so You may increase, let me sink so You may rise above. Ride forth upon me as You rode into Jerusalem on a humble little animal, a colt, the foal of a donkey, and let me hear the children cry to You, "Hosanna in the highest."

Study Guide

The author suggests that our problems stem from a "deep moral disorder" in our relationship with God. How do you see this playing out in your own life or in society?

> " We must start with God. We are right when and only when we stand in the right position relative to God, and we are wrong as far and as long as we stand in any other position."

What does it mean to you to "start with God"? How might this principle change your approach to various aspects of life?

Read Isaiah 6:1-8. How does Isaiah's vision illustrate the proper Creator-creature relation? What can we learn from his response?

Examine your various relationships (with God, others, possessions, etc.). Are they in the right order? Make a plan to adjust any that are out of alignment.

Reflect on the idea of stepping "out of the world's parade" when we decide to exalt God above all. What challenges might this present? What benefits?

Identify areas where you're tempted to follow "the world's parade" rather than God's path. Choose one area to focus on aligning with God's will this week.

Romans 12:1-2. How does Paul describe the process of restoring our relationship with God?

The author speaks of restoring the proper Creator-creature relation. How would you describe this relation? How is it different from other types of relationships?

Examine Colossians 1:15-20. What does this passage teach us about Christ's role in restoring the Creator-creature relation?

Personal Reflection and Journal

Use this space to write your responses, insights, and experiences as you work through this study. Consider the following prompts:

- How is my understanding of the Creator-creature relationship evolving through this study?

- In what ways am I learning to exalt God above all things in my life?

- What challenges am I facing in stepping out of "the world's parade"?

"Lord, I exalt You above all things in my life. Help me to consistently put You in Your rightful place. Show me any areas where I've displaced You from the center of my life. Give me the courage to restore You to Your proper position. Teach me what it means to live as a creature in right relationship with my Creator. Transform my perspective and priorities."

Meekness and Rest

Blessed are the meek: for they shall inherit the earth. Matt. 5:5

A pretty accurate description of the human race might be given to someone who doesn't know it by taking the Beatitudes, turning them inside out and saying, "Here's your human race." The exact opposites of the virtues in the Beatitudes are the very qualities that mark human life and behavior.

In the world of people, we find nothing like the virtues Jesus talked about at the start of the famous Sermon on the Mount. Instead of being poor in spirit, we find the worst kind of pride; instead of mourners, we find pleasure seekers; instead of meekness, arrogance; instead of hunger for righteousness, we hear people saying, "I'm rich and have plenty and don't need anything"; instead of mercy, we find cruelty; instead of pure hearts, corrupt thoughts; instead of peacemakers, we find people quarrelsome and resentful; instead of rejoicing in mistreatment, we find them fighting back with every weapon they have.

This is the kind of moral stuff civilized society is made of. The air is full of it; we breathe it with every breath and drink it with our mother's milk. Culture and education smooth these things out a bit but leave them basically unchanged. A whole world of literature has been created to justify this kind of life as the only normal one. And this is even more surprising since these are the evils that make life such a bitter struggle for all of us. All our heartaches and many of our physical problems come directly from our sins. Pride, arrogance, resentfulness, evil thoughts, malice, greed: these cause more human pain than all the diseases that ever troubled human flesh.

Into a world like this, the sound of Jesus' words comes wonderful and strange, like a visit from above. It's good that He spoke, for no one else could have done it as well; and it's good that we listen. His words are the essence of truth. He's not offering an opinion; Jesus never gave opinions. He never guessed; He knew, and He knows. His words aren't like Solomon's, the sum of good wisdom or the results of keen observation. He spoke out of the fullness of His Godhead, and His words are Truth itself. He's the only one who could say "blessed" with complete authority, for He is the Blessed One come from the world above to give blessedness to mankind. And His words were backed up by deeds mightier than any done on this earth by any other person. It's wise for us to listen.

As was often the case with Jesus, He used this word "meek" in a short, crisp sentence, and only later did He go on to explain it. In the same book of Matthew, He tells us more about it and applies it to our lives. "Come to me, all you who are weary and burdened, and I will give you rest. Take my yoke upon you and learn from me, for I am gentle and humble in heart, and you will find rest for your souls. For my yoke is easy and my burden is light." Here we have two things contrasting each other, a burden and a rest. The burden isn't a local one, specific to those first listeners, but one that's carried by the whole human race. It's not made up of political oppression or poverty or hard work. It's much deeper than that. It's felt by the rich as well as the poor because it's something that wealth and idleness can never free us from.

The burden carried by mankind is a heavy and crushing thing. The word Jesus used means a load carried or work done to the point of exhaustion. Rest is simply release from that burden. It's not something we do, it's what comes to us when we stop doing. His own gentleness, that is the rest.

Let's look at our burden. It's entirely an inner one. It attacks the heart and mind and only reaches the body from inside. First, there's the burden of pride. The work of self-love is really heavy. Think about whether much of your sadness hasn't come from someone speaking badly of you. As long as you set yourself up as a little god you must be loyal to, there will be those who enjoy insulting your idol. How can you hope to have inner peace then? The heart's fierce effort to protect itself from every slight, to shield its sensitive honor from the bad opinion of friend and enemy, will never let the mind rest. Keep up this fight for years and the burden will become unbearable. Yet people of the world carry this burden all the time, challenging every word spoken against them, cringing under every criticism, hurting under each imagined slight, lying awake if another is preferred before them.

This kind of burden isn't necessary to bear. Jesus calls us to His rest, and meekness is His way. The meek person doesn't care at all who is greater than he, because he decided long ago that the world's respect isn't worth the effort. He develops a kind sense of humor about himself and learns to say, "Oh, so you've been overlooked? They've put someone else before you? They've whispered that you're not really all that important after all? And now you feel hurt because the world is saying about you the very things you've been saying about yourself? Just yesterday you were telling God that you were nothing, just a worm of the dust. Where's your consistency? Come on, humble yourself, and stop caring what people think."

The meek man is not a human mouse afflicted with a sense of his own inferiority. Rather he may be in his moral life as bold as a lion and as strong as Samson; but he has stopped being fooled about himself. He's accepted God's view of his own life. He knows he's as weak and helpless as God has said he is, but strangely, he knows at the same time that in God's eyes he's more important than angels. In himself, nothing; in God, everything.

That's his motto. He knows well that the world will never see him as God sees him and he's stopped caring. He's perfectly content to let God set His own values. He'll be patient to wait for the day when everything will get its own price tag and real worth will come into its own. Then the righteous will shine in their Father's Kingdom. He's willing to wait for that day.

Meanwhile, he'll have reached a place of soul rest. As he walks on in meekness, he'll be happy to let God defend him. The old struggle to defend himself is over. He's found the peace that meekness brings.

Then he'll also be freed from the burden of pretending. By this I don't mean being fake, but the common human desire to put our best foot forward and hide our real inner poverty from the world. Sin has played many evil tricks on us, and one has been putting a false sense of shame in us. There's hardly anyone who dares to be just what they are without fixing up the impression. The fear of being found out gnaws at their hearts like rats. The cultured person is haunted by the fear that he'll someday meet someone more cultured than himself. The learned person fears meeting someone more learned than he. The rich person sweats under the fear that his clothes or car or house will someday look cheap compared to those of another rich person. So-called "society" runs on a motivation no higher than this, and the poorer classes at their level are little better.

Let no one brush this off. These burdens are real, and bit by bit they kill the victims of this harmful and unnatural way of life. And the mindset created by years of this makes true meekness seem as unreal as a dream, as distant as a star. To all the victims of this gnawing disease, Jesus says, "You must become like little children." Little children don't compare; they enjoy what they have directly without relating it to something or someone else. Only as they get older and sin starts to stir in their hearts do jealousy and envy appear. Then they can't enjoy what they have if someone else has something bigger or better. At that early age, the galling burden comes down on their tender souls, and it never leaves them until Jesus sets them free.

Another source of burden is pretending. I'm sure most people live in secret fear that someday they'll be careless and by chance an enemy or friend will be allowed to peek into their poor empty souls. So they're never relaxed. Smart people are tense and alert, afraid they might be trapped into saying something common or stupid. Well-traveled people are afraid they might meet some Marco Polo who can describe a remote place they've never been.

This unnatural state is part of our sad inheritance of sin, but today it's made worse by our whole way of life. Advertising is largely based on this habit of pretense. "Courses" are offered in this or that field of learning, openly appealing to the victim's desire to shine at a party. Books are sold, clothes and cosmetics are peddled, by constantly playing on this desire to appear what we're not. Pretending is one curse that will fall away the moment we kneel at Jesus' feet and surrender to His meekness. Then we won't care what people think of us as long as God is pleased. Then what we are will be everything; what we appear will become far less important to us. Apart from sin, we have nothing to be ashamed of. Only an evil desire to shine makes us want to appear other than we are.

The world's heart is breaking under this load of pride and pretense. There's no release from our burden apart from Christ's meekness. Good sharp reasoning might help a little, but this vice is so strong that if we push it down in one place, it will come up somewhere else. To people everywhere, Jesus says, "Come to me, and I will give you rest." The rest He offers is the rest of meekness, the blessed relief that comes when we accept ourselves for what we are and stop pretending. It will take some courage at first, but the needed grace will come as we learn that we're sharing this new and easy yoke with the strong Son of God Himself. He calls it "my yoke," and He walks at one end while we walk at the other.

Lord, make me childlike. Free me from the urge to compete with others for place or prestige or position. I want to be simple and natural as a little child. Free me from pose and pretense. Forgive me for thinking of myself. Help me forget myself and find my true peace in looking at You. So that You might answer this prayer, I humble myself before You. Put on me Your easy yoke of self-forgetfulness so that through it I may find rest. Amen.

Study Guide

Think about the paradox of being "weak and helpless" yet "of more importance than angels." How does this perspective impact your self-view?

Reflect on your reactions to criticism, praise, and challenges. How do these align with the concept of meekness presented in this chapter? Choose one area to focus on developing meekness this week.

The author describes a burden that crushes mankind. What burdens do you carry that might be relieved by embracing meekness?

> "The burden carried by mankind is a heavy and crushing thing. The word Jesus used means a load carried or work done to the point of exhaustion. Rest is simply release from that burden. It's not something we do, it's what comes to us when we stop doing."

How do you understand the concept of finding rest as not being something you do but stop doing? How can you apply this to your life?

Read Numbers 12:3 and Matthew 11:28-30. How do these passages illuminate the connection between meekness and rest?

Choose a task or responsibility that usually feels burdensome. Approach it this week with an attitude of meekness and rest in God.

"The meek man is not a human mouse afflicted with a sense of his own inferiority. Rather he may be in his moral life as bold as a lion and as strong as Samson; but he has stopped being fooled about himself."

The author suggests that a meek man is no longer fooled about himself. In what ways might you be fooled about yourself?

Study Philippians 2:5-11. How does Christ exemplify meekness?

Examine Isaiah 40:28-31. How does this passage describe the rest that God offers? How might this relate to meekness?

Personal Reflection and Journal

Use this space to write your responses, insights, and experiences as you work through this study. Consider the following prompts:

- In what ways am I experiencing God's rest as I practice meekness?

- What challenges am I facing in embracing true meekness in my daily life?

- How is the practice of meekness impacting my relationship with God and others?

"Lord, teach me true meekness. Help me to see myself as You see me, neither more nor less. I bring my burdens to You. Show me how to find rest in Your meekness and gentleness. Transform my understanding of strength and weakness. Let me find my true identity and rest in Christ."

The Sacrament of Living

Therefore, whether you eat or drink, or whatever you do, do all to the glory of God. I Cor. 10:31

One of the biggest obstacles to inner peace that Christians face is the common habit of splitting our lives into two areas: the sacred and the secular. We think of these areas as separate and morally and spiritually incompatible. Since we're forced by life's necessities to constantly move back and forth between them, our inner lives tend to break apart. We end up living a divided life instead of a unified one.

Our problem comes from the fact that we who follow Christ live in two worlds at once, the spiritual and the natural. As children of Adam, we live on earth limited by our physical bodies and subject to human weaknesses and illnesses. Just living among people requires years of hard work and much care and attention to worldly things. In stark contrast to this is our spiritual life. There we enjoy a different and higher kind of life; we're children of God, we have heavenly status and enjoy close fellowship with Christ.

This tends to split our life into two parts. We unconsciously start to recognize two types of actions. The first are done with a feeling of satisfaction and a strong belief that they please God. These are the sacred acts and they're usually thought to be prayer, Bible reading, singing hymns, going to church, and other acts that come directly from faith. We can recognize them because they have no direct connection to this world and would have no meaning except that faith shows us another world, "a house not made with hands, eternal in the heavens."

Opposite these sacred acts are the secular ones. These include all the ordinary activities of life that we share with other people: eating, sleeping, working, taking care of our bodies, and doing our dull and ordinary duties here on earth. We often do these reluctantly and with many doubts, often apologizing to God for what we consider a waste of time and energy. The result is that we're uneasy most of the time. We do our common tasks feeling deeply frustrated, telling ourselves sadly that a better day is coming when we'll shed this earthly shell and no longer be bothered with worldly affairs.

This is the old sacred-secular divide. Most Christians are caught in its trap. They can't find a satisfactory balance between the demands of the two worlds. They try to walk a tightrope between two kingdoms and find no peace in either. Their strength is reduced, their outlook confused, and their joy taken away.

I believe this situation is completely unnecessary. We've gotten ourselves into a dilemma, true, but the dilemma isn't real. It's created by misunderstanding. The divide has no basis in the New Testament. Without doubt, a better understanding of Christian truth will free us from it.

The Lord Jesus Christ Himself is our perfect example, and He knew no divided life. In His Father's Presence, He lived on earth without strain from babyhood to His death on the cross. God accepted the offering of His whole life and made no distinction between one act and another. "I always do what pleases him," was His brief summary of His own life in relation to the Father. As He moved among people, He was calm and at peace. The pressure and suffering He endured came from His position as the world's sin bearer; they were never the result of moral uncertainty or spiritual maladjustment.

Paul's advice to "do all to the glory of God" is more than just a nice idea. It's an important part of sacred teaching and should be accepted as the Word of Truth. It opens up the possibility of making every act in our lives contribute to God's glory. In case we might be too shy to include everything, Paul specifically mentions eating and drinking. This basic activity we share with animals. If these simple animal acts can be done in a way that honors God, then it's hard to think of any act that can't.

That monk-like hatred of the body that's so common in some early devotional writings has no support in God's Word. The Bible does talk about modesty, it's true, but never prudishness or a false sense of shame. The New Testament accepts as a fact that when Jesus became human, He took on a real human body, and no effort is made to avoid the clear implications of this fact. He lived in that body here among people and never once did a non-sacred act. His presence in human flesh forever removes the wrong idea that there's something inherently offensive to God about the human body. God created our bodies, and we don't offend Him by placing the responsibility where it belongs. He's not ashamed of the work of His own hands.

Misuse and abuse of our human powers should give us enough reason to be ashamed. Bodily acts done in sin and against nature can never honor God. Wherever human will introduces moral evil, we no longer have our innocent and harmless powers as God made them; instead, we have a misused and twisted thing that can never bring glory to its Creator.

Let's assume, however, that misuse and abuse aren't present. Let's think of a Christian believer who has experienced the twin wonders of repentance and new birth. They're now living according to God's will as they understand it from the Bible. For such a person, it can be said that every act of their life is or can be as truly sacred as prayer or baptism or the Lord's Supper. To say this isn't to bring all acts down to one dead level; it's rather to lift every act up into a living kingdom and turn the whole life into a sacrament.

If a sacrament is an outward expression of an inward grace, then we needn't hesitate to accept this idea. By one act of dedicating our whole selves to God, we can make every subsequent act express that dedication. We need no more be ashamed of our body – the physical servant that carries us through life – than Jesus was of the humble donkey He rode into Jerusalem. "The Lord needs it" may well apply to our mortal bodies. If Christ lives in us, we may carry the Lord of glory as that little animal did long ago and give reason for the crowds to cry, "Hosanna in the highest."

Just seeing this truth isn't enough. If we want to escape from the trap of the sacred-secular divide, the truth must "run in our blood" and shape our thoughts. We must practice living to God's glory, actually and deliberately. By thinking about this truth, by talking it over with God often in our prayers, by reminding ourselves of it frequently as we move among people, a sense of its wonderful meaning will start to take hold of us. The old painful division will give way to a peaceful unity of life. The knowledge that we are all God's, that He has accepted all and rejected nothing, will unify our inner lives and make everything sacred to us.

This isn't quite everything. Long-held habits don't die easily. It will take smart thinking and a lot of respectful prayer to completely escape from the sacred-secular way of thinking. For example, it might be hard for the average Christian to grasp the idea that their daily work can be done as acts of worship acceptable to God through Jesus Christ. The old division will sometimes pop up in the back of their mind to disturb their peace. And the devil won't take all this lying down. He'll be there in the car or at the desk or in the field to remind the Christian that they're giving most of their day to worldly things and only a tiny bit of time to religious duties. Unless great care is taken, this will create confusion and bring discouragement and heaviness of heart.

We can only meet this successfully by using strong faith. We must offer all our acts to God and believe that He accepts them. Then hold firmly to that position and keep insisting that every act of every hour of the day and night be included in this. Keep reminding God in our private prayer times that we mean every act for His glory; then add to those times with a thousand thought-prayers as we go about living. Let's practice the fine art of making every work a priestly service. Let's believe that God is in all our simple deeds and learn to find Him there.

A related error to what we've been discussing is applying the sacred-secular divide to places. It's amazing that we can read the New Testament and still believe in the inherent sacredness of some places as different from others. This error is so widespread that one feels all alone when trying to fight it. It has acted like a dye, coloring the thinking of religious people and even coloring their eyes so that it's almost impossible to see its mistake. Despite every New Testament teaching against it, it has been said and sung for centuries and accepted as part of the Christian message, which it certainly is not. Only the Quakers, as far as I know, have had the insight to see the error and the courage to expose it.

Here are the facts as I see them. For four hundred years Israel had lived in Egypt, surrounded by the crudest idolatry. Moses led them out at last and started them toward the promised land. They had lost the very idea of holiness. To correct this, God started at the bottom. He localized Himself in the cloud and fire and later, when the tabernacle was built, He lived in fiery display in the Most Holy Place. Through countless distinctions, God taught Israel the difference between holy and unholy. There were holy days, holy vessels, holy clothes. There were washings, sacrifices, offerings of many kinds. Through these means, Israel learned that God is holy. This was what He was teaching them. Not the holiness of things or places, but the holiness of God was the lesson they had to learn.

Then came the great day when Christ appeared. Right away He began to say, "You have heard that it was said to the people long ago—but I tell you." The Old Testament schooling was over. When Christ died on the cross, the temple curtain was torn from top to bottom. The Most Holy Place was opened to everyone who would enter in faith. Christ's words were remembered, "A time is coming when you will worship the Father neither on this mountain nor in Jerusalem... Yet a time is coming and has now come when the true worshipers will worship the Father in the Spirit and in truth, for they are the kind of worshipers the Father seeks. God is spirit, and his worshipers must worship in the Spirit and in truth."

Soon after, Paul took up the call for freedom and declared all foods clean, every day holy, all places sacred, and every act acceptable to God. The sacredness of specific times and places, a partial light needed to educate people, faded away before the full sun of spiritual worship.

The essential spirituality of worship stayed with the Church until it was slowly lost over the years. Then the natural tendency of fallen human hearts to make rules began to bring back the old distinctions. The Church started again to observe special days and seasons and times. Certain places were chosen and marked as holy in a special way. Differences were noted between one day or place or person and another. "The sacraments" were first two, then three, then four until with the triumph of Roman Catholicism they were set at seven.

In all kindness, and with no wish to speak badly of any Christian, however misguided, I'd point out that the Roman Catholic church today represents the sacred-secular mistake carried to its logical end. Its worst effect is the complete split it creates between religion and life. Its teachers try to avoid this trap with many footnotes and explanations, but the mind's instinct for logic is too strong. In everyday living, the split is a fact.

Reformers and puritans and mystics have worked to free us from this bondage. Today, the trend in conservative circles is back toward that bondage again. It's said that a horse, after being led out of a burning building, will sometimes strangely break free from its rescuer and run back into the building to die in the flames. By some such stubborn tendency toward error, Fundamentalism in our day is moving back toward spiritual slavery. The observance of special days and times is becoming more and more common among us. "Lent" and "holy week" and "Good Friday" are words heard more and more often from gospel Christians. We don't know when we're well off.

So that I'm understood and not misunderstood, I'd like to highlight the practical implications of what I've been arguing for, that is, the sacramental quality of everyday living. Against its positive meanings, I'd like to point out a few things it doesn't mean.

This doesn't mean, for instance, that everything we do is equally important. One act in a good person's life might be much more important than another. Paul's tent-making wasn't as important as his writing of the Letter to the Romans, but both were accepted by God and both were true acts of worship. Certainly, leading someone to Christ is more important than planting a garden, but planting the garden can be just as holy an act as winning a soul.

Also, it doesn't mean that every person is as useful as every other person. Gifts differ in the body of Christ. A Billy Bray can't be compared with a Luther or a Wesley for sheer usefulness to the Church and the world; but the service of the less gifted brother is as pure as that of the more gifted, and God accepts both with equal pleasure.

The ordinary person should never think their humbler task is inferior to that of their minister. Let everyone stay in the calling where they are called and their work will be as sacred as the work of the ministry. It's not what a person does that determines whether their work is sacred or secular, it's why they do it. The motive is everything. Let a person honor the Lord God in their heart and they can thereafter do no common act. All they do is good and acceptable to God through Jesus Christ. For such a person, living itself will be sacramental and the whole world a sanctuary. Their entire life will be a priestly service. As they perform even their simplest task, they will hear the voice of the seraphim saying, "Holy, Holy, Holy, is the Lord of hosts: the whole earth is full of his glory."

Lord, I would trust You completely; I would be entirely Yours; I would exalt You above all. I want to feel no sense of owning anything outside of You. I want to be constantly aware of Your overshadowing Presence and to hear Your speaking Voice. I long to live in restful sincerity of heart. I want to live so fully in the Spirit that all my thoughts may be like sweet incense rising to You and every act of my life may be an act of worship. Therefore I pray in the words of Your great servant of old, "I beg You so to cleanse the intent of my heart with the unspeakable gift of Your grace, that I may perfectly love You and worthily praise You." And all this I confidently believe You will grant me through the merits of Jesus Christ Your Son. Amen.

Study Guide

The author suggests that all of life can be sacred. How might this perspective change your approach to everyday tasks?

Reflect on the statement, " It's not what a person does that determines whether their work is sacred or secular, it's why they do it. The motive is everything." How does this challenge or affirm your view of work and service?

List your daily activities and reflect on how each could be viewed as sacred.

Read Colossians 3:17,23-24. How do these verses relate to the theme of the chapter? What do they teach about the integration of faith and daily life?

How do you understand the concept of doing everything "to the glory of God"? What challenges might this present in your life?

The author speaks of life as a sacrament. How might viewing all of life as sacred transform your spiritual journey?

Examine Romans 12:1-2. How does Paul's concept of "living sacrifice" relate to the idea of all life being sacred?

Choose one "secular" task you do regularly. For a week, approach it as a sacred act, offering it to God. Journal about how this changes your experience of the task.

Personal Reflection and Journal

Use this space to write your responses, insights, and experiences as you work through this study. Consider the following prompts:

- In what ways am I learning to see all of life as an opportunity for worship?

- What challenges am I facing in breaking down the sacred-secular divide in my life?

- How is the practice of viewing all life as sacred impacting my relationship with God and others?

"Lord, help me to see all aspects of my life as sacred. Transform my perspective on the ordinary tasks of my day. I offer all my activities to You as acts of worship. Show me how to glorify You in everything I do. Break down the artificial barriers I've created between sacred and secular in my life. Teach me to live wholly for You."

About the author

Aiden Wilson Tozer (1897-1963) was an American Christian pastor, preacher, author, magazine editor, and spiritual mentor. Born on a small farm in western Pennsylvania, Tozer had little formal education but became one of the most influential voices in Christian thought during the mid-20th century.

Tozer was converted to Christianity as a teenager and began preaching soon after. He served as a pastor in the Christian and Missionary Alliance church for over 30 years, most notably at the Southside Alliance Church in Chicago from 1928 to 1959.

Known for his deep spiritual insight and poignant writing style, Tozer authored more than 40 books, with "The Pursuit of God" and "The Knowledge of the Holy" being his most widely recognized works. He was also the editor of "The Alliance Weekly" magazine for many years.

Tozer's teachings emphasized the importance of a deeper life in Christ, personal holiness, and the pursuit of God. His works continue to influence Christians across denominational lines long after his death.

Made in the USA
Monee, IL
04 February 2025